NATURAL RE
SECRETS TO ST

T0096214

# THE
# ENERGETICS
## OF JOY

## DR. MICHELLE
## **EGGENBERGER**
### PREMA OM

Difference Press

McLean, Virginia, USA

Published 2019

ISBN: 978-1-68309-230-8

DISCLAIMER

Cover Design: Jennifer Stimson

Editor: Bethany Davis

Author Photo Credit: Jenn Reid

DEDICATED TO
My beloved Anis and all who are suffering.
May you be Happy, Peaceful and Free!

# TABLE OF CONTENTS

# Introduction

For over ten years now, I have had the privilege to treat patients from all over the world with all types of conditions. From migraines to infertility, from chronic back pains to fibromyalgia, you name it! Usually when people have come to me they have already tried all the "traditional" approaches conventional medicine has to offer with no true relief. It is because everything else has failed that they have become desperate enough to try "alternative medicine."

In fact, I am sure that you have already tried different "conventional" approaches to treat your stress and anxiety with no success, and that might be the reason why you decided to get this book in the first place. However, let me tell you, right now you are at an advantage over many others who are now suffering from chronic illnesses. Why? Because by taking action and resolving your chronic stress and anxiety, you will avoid a whole lot more suffering. Let me explain.

Over the last ten years, one thing that has become evident to me is that no matter the condition, the gender, the country, the economic status, etc., the one thing that all of my patients have had in common is an undercurrent of untreated chronic stress and anxiety.

Untreated chronic stress and anxiety disrupts the energy flow in the body, which ends up having an effect on the patient's neuroendocrine axis. This means that your hormones will be affected and over time, your nervous system and digestive system will be as well. This will disrupt the way you eat, sleep, and feel in general, provoking even more imbalance in your mental state as well, which slowly becomes a never-ending merry-go-round.

That is why at the end of each chapter I have included a client success story that begins as some type of symptom other than stress and anxiety, so you can see how address-ing stress and anxiety relieved their depression, migraine, backache etc.

By doing this, each patient experiences true healing and sometimes even powerful life transformations. You see, the body, the mind, and the Spirit are all interconnected, and addressing only one part as a separate entity will not truly address the root cause. That would be like having a hose full of holes and trying to fix one hole by covering it with a Band-Aid to, moments later, discover that two more new holes have popped up.

What you will see here are the secrets of "alternative medicine," or the original medicine that has been used for thousands of years successfully, so much so that it is still around to this day. Thankfully, more and more people are becoming receptive again to its amazing and long-lasting results. This is the medicine discovered by the sages, shamans, yogis, and highly Spiritual beings, who by going into deep communion with Nature and Source have uncovered the internal workings of the body, the mind and Spirit, and the energetic pathways that allow for this life force to flow in the body with ease and, by doing so, allowing body, mind, and Spirit to be whole!

In this book you will be gently introduced to some of these concepts and why it is important to apply them to your life in order to get rid of your stress, anxiety, and depression.

# CHAPTER ONE
## WALKING IN YOUR SHOES

*"I see you."*

– AVATAR

I'll bet it feels lonely where you are right now. I'll bet you are trying to find the words to describe exactly how you feel and there are no words to really describe that feeling. That feeling that starts in the pit of your stomach and ends up right in your throat. That feeling that sits on your chest and doesn't let you breathe or think or be. That feeling that is not just a feeling anymore. It no longer lets you sleep. It doesn't let you eat. It doesn't leave you alone. That feeling that keeps asking you to play the same questions like a broken record in your head.

"Why is this happening to me? What is wrong with me? Why am I in this situation?

Why do I feel the way I feel? Why am I not happy?"

Anxiety and depression are not something people physically see, so no one can truly understand what is going on inside of you. Even the people closest to you won't be able to put themselves in your shoes and know how difficult it is to function day in and day out with this constant feeling of having something "missing," like knowing you forgot something and you just don't know what it is or feeling a weight constantly on your shoulders or, like one of my patients said to me, feeling like "an elephant is sitting on your chest" ALL the time. In fact, dealing with this constant sense of worry makes you feel stuck, like you are in a funk.

Worry becomes a constant companion. Worry about what? Sometimes you yourself don't even know! It could be a worry about your finances, your work, your health or lack of health, your relationship or lack of it, your weight, your kids or lack of them, your house, your aging parents, your age and where you are in life, your dog... it doesn't matter. There is always something to worry about and, if there's not, THAT will also be a reason to worry, since you will worry about when the ball will fall.

As a successful, independent, high-achieving professional, there is so much for you to juggle that eventually something will fall and you know it. For years you have been managing it all, day in and day out, without complaint. You are the captain, nothing works without you overseeing and directing the ship, and you have done it to perfection, and if the ship went off course, you solved it. No problem! You are a problem solver, that is what you do. You are the person people go to solve their problems.

Yet lately, problems seem to be following you everywhere. Your job is no longer what it used to be or the pressures of it seem too much, your relationship or lack of it is making you even more stressed out and anxious, and your health seems to start suffering as well!

You have a life to live and have no time to be dealing with this anxiety and slight depression that has you paralyzed, unable to make decisions and move forward.

Yet this feeling of anxiety is starting to tint everything you do. Like a pesky fly, it won't leave you alone and the worst thing is you don't know when it will show its ugly head again.

Maybe it rears its head while you are sleeping or right before you go to sleep, making it impossible to truly rest. Maybe it will be right before you have a huge presentation. Maybe, just maybe, when you least expect it, this feeling of anxiety will come in so severely that you will think you are having a heart attack right in the middle of 5 p.m. traffic, and you'll end up having the cute EMT at the hospital give you a paper bag to breathe in, 'cause all you were having is a panic attack.

Anxiety has now managed to infiltrate all parts of your life, making it difficult to enjoy it. This nagging feeling of "Is this it? I have everything I have dreamed of. I should be happy, I should be feeling nothing but joy, and yet all I feel is apathy and a sense of worry..."

No, you are not crazy, but the constant worry sure is driving you and everyone around you crazy. They can't understand what there is to worry about. Why can't you just relax? Or maybe you are just hormonal and should get over it! Yes, why can't you just get over it? You are strong, you are a doer, you are a high achiever, you are a professional, for crying out loud – why can't you just get over it?

Funny you should ask. Anxiety and even mild depression are not things that are easy to get over, as many people, including you, think. Even your doctor, who has studied for years, doesn't know what else to do! First, he gave you meds to help you sleep better when you felt exhausted since it seemed your anxiety wasn't letting you sleep – yet you still feel like a zombie when you wake up and pretty much for the rest of the day. Then, your constant indigestion and reflux got you a free trip to his office again, this time for an endoscopy, where he got a front seat view to the cavernous nooks and crannies of your stomach and your juicy juices – fun! Thankfully, he did not find anything worth mentioning, yet he thought he would give you gastritis medication for good measure. Yes, I know you are still having reflux problems and indigestion...

Then your hair started to fall out. The occasional headache has become a migraine and your weight started to fluctuate... Well, he thought it was your thyroid, so off you went once again to get pinched and prodded, all for him to tell you that your labs were slightly off but not significantly enough to give you a specific diagnosis.

In the end he finally gave up and attributed your condition to stress. He prescribed an anxiety medication and stress management therapy, which you have been doing religiously since he prescribed it.

How is that going for you? Has it worked for you? I am sure it hasn't, 'cause you are here, reading this book. I know, it is painful to get here. You have done everything your doctor has told you to do, you even said yes when he prescribed a higher dose, but it did not work so you don't want to go that route anymore. Or maybe you haven't even tried the medication because you are afraid that if you do you will get hooked! You are frustrated and overwhelmed. You don't want to miss out on the life you have worked so hard to create, much less become addicted to prescription medication, plus deep inside you know there is more. Deep inside you know this is not the answer, yet you don't know what else to do and who to go to to get your life back.

Well, I know it is hard to see right now, but there *is* a way to be anxiety-free naturally. There is a way to enjoy your life and live it fully.

That doesn't mean that you will not have problems, nor that you won't get concerned or experience fear once in a while. Hey, fear is a fundamental human reaction and, used properly, it can be quite helpful! But there is a way to not only have a life without anxiety but a life where you are completely content and happy. A life of deep meaning and joy. A life where you get to enjoy all aspects of your life and cultivate radiant health, joy, and peace. A life worth waking up in the morning and thanking your lucky stars for at night. A life worth living!

How do I know? I know because I have walked in your shoes and it transformed my life!

# Chapter Two

## FREEING MYSELF FROM ANXIETY AND DISCOVERING MYSELF IN THE PROCESS

*"Our deepest fear is not that we are inadequate. Our deepest fear is that we are powerful beyond measure. It is our light, not our darkness that most frightens us. We ask ourselves, who am I to be brilliant, gorgeous, talented, fabulous? Actually, who are you not to be? You are a child of God. Your playing small does not serve the world. There is nothing enlightened about shrinking so that other people won't feel insecure around you. We are all meant to shine, as children do. We were born to make manifest the glory of God that is within us.*

*It's not just in some of us; it's in everyone. And as we let our own light shine, we unconsciously give other people permission to do the same. As we are liberated from our own fear, our presence automatically liberates others."*

– Marianne Williamson, *A Return to Love: Reflections on the Principles of a Course in Miracles*

I could hear the siren going on. There in that small room in the basement of the McDonald's corporation headquarters, surrounded by the who's who of this amazingly successful corporation, is when I felt it for the first time.

As a female Associate Creative Director of one of the most successful Hispanic advertising agencies in the US, I was finally invited to present one of our advertising campaigns to the top marketing director of McDonald's. She oversaw the advertising campaigns worldwide and, for the first time ever, I was finally going to present to her and her team.

Just as we were getting ready to start the presentation, the siren went off and we were all rushed to a small room in the basement of the building, since it seemed a tornado was coming our way.

Everybody seemed anxious, except me. I... I couldn't believe it. I, Michelle, this little girl from Guatemala, had finally made it. As I looked around the room I could not only see the top dogs of this amazing advertising agency, but the top dogs of this worldwide brand recognized all over the world for its success! I was about to present one of *my* ideas to these amazing business people, and for a second I felt so proud, so fulfilled... and then it hit me... a deep sense of emptiness, of deep sadness and, like a bubble about to burst, a thought popped into my head: "Is this it?!" Is this what success feels like? Is this what I have been dreaming about?

I felt this pressure in my chest and it got slightly difficulty to breathe. The siren stopped, and we went back to the conference room. My idea got approved, and that was the first of many other presentations and many other bursts of anxiety.

As my traveling here and there for presentations, commercials, and award ceremonies intensified, so did my discontent, my sense of emptiness, and my anxiety. I was constantly fighting with my fellow teammates about which idea was better and who got to present and get recognition, and I always felt like I got the short end of the stick (that was my ego, by the way... we will get into that later). My relationship with my boss was not the best and he sure made it hard for me to show all "my talents and potential" – well, that's what I thought (again, my ego).

At the same time, personally, it seemed I just couldn't find the right guy for me. After having a devastating relationship with a very fun, good looking, womanizer colleague of mine, he had finally had it with my jealousy and neediness and I had finally had it with his womanizing and partying. I decided to break it off. The fear of losing him, finally losing him, and the fear of not finding love again made me frantically go to the gym, eat very little, smoke even more, party, and spend tons and tons of money on clothes, salons, and spas, only to have the relationship almost mimic itself completely with every new guy I met afterwards.

Plus, to add to it all, I started to get sick. I was catching colds frequently, that later became bronchitis, which finally was diagnosed as asthma.

"Why is this happening to me? What is wrong with me? Why am I in this situation? Why do I feel like I feel? Why I am not happy?" These same questions started playing in my head like a broken record, causing me deep anxiety to the point of ending up at the hospital with a panic attack.

I had everything I ever wanted, a great career, an apartment with water views, an expensive car, a new relationship, money... yet I wasn't happy. I was stressed and anxious all the time. I didn't sleep well, and I had this nagging feeling that something was missing.

I was so incredibly unhappy, so in pain, that I knew I had to do something. I knew I had to find an answer to my health problems, to my borderline depression and my overall sense of worry. Never in my wildest dreams did I think that finally saying *enough* would take me into such a different direction.

I was blessed to bump into the book *The Art of Happiness* by the Dalai Lama in the airport on one of my business trips, which ignited something very profound within me. It opened my mind to the possibility of the idea of happiness as something completely different than I had ever heard of or known. At the same time, in the magical synergistic ways of the Universe my doctor, tired of hearing me complain about my asthma, gave me his final sentence: "Michelle, you will have to be on steroids and inhalers for the rest of your life." I wasn't even thirty!

It was then that I finally decided to take real ownership of my health, my anxiety, and my unhappiness and started looking for alternative ways to do so.

I was guided by a friend to try acupuncture, which I did, and following my new interest in Eastern philosophies, plus the fact that the women who did it seemed to have amazing bodies, I decided to give yoga a go and went on a five-day retreat for yoga and writing in Costa Rica. So my life transformation began.

A year later, I had stopped smoking and was asthma-free. I thought, wow, if I can do this for someone else, this is what I want to do!

I signed up for a Master's in Traditional Chinese Medicine, without knowing exactly how I was going to pay for it or how I was going to find the time, but something deep inside of me told me it was the beginning of the life I was truly meant to live.

I tell you, when you are aligned with your purpose, when you decide to stop fighting life and trying to force it into what you think it should be, and instead become receptive to Grace and all the wonderful gifts it has prepared for you, the impossible can happen!

I, who had been so attached to my BMW, my apartment on the bay, my expensive clothes, salons, and spas, gave it all up happily.

I changed my BMW out for a Toyota Yaris, rented my nice apartment out, and had the blessing of one of the angels that the Universe sent to me to rent me a room in her house, which was minutes away from the college where I was studying, making it very convenient for me, especially because classes ended at 10 p.m.

I stopped spending money on partying, cigarettes, expensive clothes, spas, and salons and was able to pay for my new career and save!

Because I knew I had to leave by 6 at the latest so I could start school at 6:30 p.m., I became super productive at work. I no longer had time to focus on my ego, on how people were not giving me the recognition I deserved, or on how cool or not cool my ideas were. I was solely focused on the work and that was it.

Saturdays were spent in clinic seeing patients, supervised by our teachers, and Sundays were spent studying for board exams.

I was working and studying full time.

Incredibly, things at work started to go a lot more smoothly and I found such joy and purpose in clinic, focusing on someone else's pain and what I could do to help.

Four difficult, exhausting, and life-changing years passed and through it all I had learned how to take better care of my body based on the principles of Traditional Chinese Medicine and yoga. I had learned what foods, herbs, and supplements could support me, new therapies that could realign my energy and keep my body flexible and supple, and, most importantly, I discovered new techniques to deal with my stress and see life in a completely new light.

I had finally finished my studies and, after working for over ten years at the advertising agency, I was finally ready to take a vacation. I decided to learn more about the Real Self, meditation, and yoga so I could give more tools to my patients in the future. I decided to ask for my four-week vacation from work all at once to do my month-long 200-hour yoga teacher certification immersion at Kripalu Center. And although I had requested this vacation months in advance and had gotten the approval of my boss, the day before my departure one of the agency owner's right hand came to ask me to stay and help out with a big presentation that had come up. I was afraid. I still did not have my US residency, which I had been waiting eight years for and which could be only offered through the company, meaning that without the job I could lose my chance to stay in the US. Yet I knew at that moment that I had a choice. I could choose the perceived safety of a job that no longer fit me and the financial luxuries it provided, or I could be fearless and jump into the unknown, following my heart and trusting that the same power that had sustained me through the challenges of lack of time, financial difficulties, and tough work over the last four years would do so again. Although I was terrified... I chose to jump! I excused myself and chose to leave for Kripalu under the ultimatum that my job could suffer because of it.

Two weeks had passed after my return from Kripalu. I was still at work when all of a sudden, I received a call. It was my immigration lawyer; my residency had been approved. I was free! I could not believe it! I quickly opened my email to let my parents know. I saw two emails. The first one was a letter from the Florida Department of Health. I had passed my boards and I was now a Licensed Acupuncture Physician. The second email was from a medical doctor who had heard about me from a patient I had treated at the student clinic. He wanted to offer me a job.

It was too much! I could not believe how everything was working out so perfectly, when I saw my boss come into the office. He quickly said my name and walked me straight to his office.

I was walking back to my cubicle from my boss' office when I saw my work partner, who solemnly looked at me and asked, "So?" "They let me go," I said.

He was about to tell me how sorry he was when I started laughing and gave him the biggest hug. "They let me go!"

Because they let me go without a reason to do so other that they had lost an account I was not even part of, they had to pay me severance *and* they could not charge me the thousands of dollars the legal residency process had cost, because I had not broken our contract, *plus* it made it easy for me to go into the next chapter of my life. I had money to open my practice, money to sustain me for the next six months while it grew, and I left with a sense of peace and infinite gratitude in my heart.

You see, at the moment when I started this whole new journey, I thought it was my asthma that was the problem and what pushed me to action. But deep inside it was my stress, anxiety, and depression about living a life that no longer fit me that had caused me so much suffering (physically, mentally, and Spiritually). It was the pain of the medical condition that pushed me, like many of my patients and clients, to take action, to finally do something about a life I was not happy with. And although deep inside I had known for a long time I was not happy, I didn't have the insight and courage to admit it to myself.

Plus, it gave me the gift of learning the importance of my body's energy and, most importantly, how by changing myself from the inside out, I could change my life in a meaningful way.

No awards, no recognition, no relationship, no amount of money or material things can ever compare to the joy I experience when I go to bed tired, knowing that someone breathed a little easier today because I dared to trust in the loving kindness of Grace.

Since then, I have become a Doctor of Traditional Chinese Medicine, Health Coach, Certified Yoga Instructor, and author, and I have had the honor of successfully treating and teaching people in the US, Australia, and Central America.

If you are ready and willing, I will be happy to show you how you, too, can become fearless and not only live free from anxiety but connect to that which will give you a sense of purpose and guide you into living the life you were meant to live!

# Chapter Three

## COMING OUT OF THE DARK

*"Just when the caterpillar thought the world was over, it became a butterfly..."*

– Anonymous

For over ten years now I have been treating patients who suffer from conditions as challenging as migraines, depression, chronic back pain, infertility, autoimmune conditions, heart conditions, cancer, etc. and at the center of them all is untreated anxiety and even depression.

Anxiety can cause an inexplicable amount of pain mentally, emotionally, and eventually physically. I know that you are experiencing it right now, and I can't tell you how much I wish you were not.

However, I would like to share the following story with you. I read it while I was going through the most challenging part of my story with anxiety and depression and it helped me tremendously in understanding that pain sometimes is exactly what we need in order to become the person we are meant to be. The story goes like this:

*A man found a cocoon of a butterfly.*

*One day a small opening appeared. He sat and watched the butterfly for several hours as it struggled to force its body through that little hole.*

*Then it seemed to stop making any progress. It appeared as if it had gotten as far as it could and it could go no farther.*

*So the man decided to help the butterfly, he took a pair of scissors and snipped off the remaining bit of the cocoon.*

*The butterfly then emerged easily.*

*But it had a swollen body and small, shriveled wings.*

*The man continued to watch the butterfly because he expected that, any moment, the wings would enlarge and expand to be able to support the body, which would contract in time.*

*Neither happened!*

*In fact, the butterfly spent the rest of its life crawling*
*around with a swollen body and shriveled wings.*
*It never was able to fly.*
*What the man in his kindness and haste did not understand*
*was that the restricting cocoon and the struggle required*
*for the butterfly to get through the tiny opening were*
*nature's way of forcing fluid from the body of the butterfly*
*into its wings so that it would be ready for flight once*
*it achieved its freedom from the cocoon.*
*Sometimes struggles are exactly what we need in our life.*
*If we went through our life without any obstacles, it*
*would cripple us. We would not be as strong*
*as what we could have been. And we could never fly.*
*So when you are under pressure and stress, remember*
*that you are a better person after you have gone through it.*

– Author Unknown

As you see, pain can be a great catalyst for change if we are ready for the challenge and believe me, my darling, YOU ARE. You are here, you are reading this book, you have fought the fight and now it is time to do it for the last time.

You will become so much healthier, stronger, and more purposeful once you have overcome!

Being able to tackle your anxiety and depression straight on and being willing to go deep will help you live a much healthier life – and who knows, maybe, just like me, it could actually become your compass into discovering your life's purpose.

In this book you will find secrets that have been used successfully for thousands of years put into a program that combines not only what I have learned in my personal experience over twenty years, but what I have used with my patients and students, which has helped them not only feel better but thrive!

## Secret One – Mass Hallucination

By practicing the first secret of the program, you will develop the awareness needed to recognize what the conditions are that are fostering chronic stress and anxiety in your life and how, by recognizing them first, you will be able to correct them.

## Secret Two – Acceptance and Self-Love

By practicing the second secret of the program, you will

learn what anxiety is truly about and what you need to anchor yourself to in order to create long-lasting change that will allow you to transform your anxiety forever.

## Secret Three – Generating Energy

By practicing the third secret of the program, you will learn how anxiety manifests in the body and how you can tap into your own healing powers to support and nurture your body and mind.

## Secret Four – Imagination vs Reality

By practicing the fourth secret of the program, you will learn to recognize thoughts and beliefs that no longer serve you and you will learn new ones that will support you in creating the life you envision for yourself.

## Secret Five – Changing the World

By practicing the fifth secret of the program, you will understand the deeper meaning of your search and you will develop a profound urgency to find it.

These are the five secrets that helped me and many of my patients to become free of anxiety, depression, and physical ailments while at the same time reigniting the fire within and making MAGIC!

As you read the book, you will discover that there are concepts and exercises that will be required to be visited again and again, and their meanings will become deeper and deeper the more you put them into practice and the deeper your understanding becomes.

Also, although each chapter stands on its own, I recommend reading the book from the beginning to end first and then focusing on the chapters you need more work on or the ones that resonate with you most at the time.

So, do not wait until it is too late, when you have already developed another medical condition or when the pain you are suffering is even greater. Start putting what you have learned into practice now. Today is the day to start your new life. Today is all we have got, so now is the time, for it is all we have!

Please know that I am always here for you if you have any questions or if you would like to be guided through the program until you can fly with your own beautiful butterfly wings!

You can reach me at **info@theenergeticsofjoy.com**.

# CHAPTER FOUR

## SECRET ONE – "MASS HALLUCINATION"

A rare conversation between Ramkrishna Paramahansa & Swami Vivekananda is one of the best messages I have come across.

> **Swami Vivekanand:** *I can't find free time.*
> *Life has become hectic.*

> **Ramkrishna Paramahansa:** *Activity gets you busy.*
> *But productivity gets you free.*

> **Swami Vivekanand:**
> *Why has life become complicated now?*

**Ramkrishna Paramahansa:**

*Stop analyzing life. It makes it complicated. Just live it.*

**Swami Vivekanand:**

*Why are we then constantly unhappy?*

**Ramkrishna Paramahansa:**

*Worrying has become your habit.*
*That's why you are not happy.*

**Swami Vivekanand:** *Why do good people always suffer?*

**Ramkrishna Paramahansa:** *Diamond cannot be polished*
*without friction. Gold cannot be purified without fire.*
*Good people go through trials, but don't suffer.*
*With that experience their life becomes better, not bitter.*

**Swami Vivekanand:**

*You mean to say such experience is useful?*

**Ramkrishna Paramahansa:** *Yes. In every term, Experience*
*is a hard teacher. She gives the test first and then lessons.*

**Swami Vivekanand:** *Because of so many problems, we don't*
*know where we are heading....*

*Ramkrishna Paramahansa: If you look outside you will not know where you are heading. Look inside. Eyes provide sight. Heart provides the way.*

*Swami Vivekanand: Does failure hurt more than moving in the right direction?*

*Ramkrishna Paramahansa: Success is a measure as decided by others. Satisfaction is a measure as decided by you.*

*Swami Vivekanand: In tough times, how do you stay motivated?*

*Ramkrishna Paramahansa: Always look at how far you have come rather than how far you have to go. Always count your blessings, not what you are missing.*

*Swami Vivekanand: What surprises you about people?*

*Ramkrishna Paramahansa: When they suffer they ask, "Why me?" When they prosper, they never ask, "Why me?"*

*Swami Vivekanand: How can I get the best out of life?*

*Ramkrishna Paramahansa: Face your past without regret. Handle your present with confidence. Prepare for the future without fear.*

*Swami Vivekanand: One last question.*
*Sometimes I feel my prayers are not answered.*

*Ramkrishna Paramahansa: There are no unanswered*
*prayers. Keep the faith and drop the fear. Life is a mystery to*
*solve, not a problem to resolve. Trust me. Life is wonderful*
*if you know how to live.*

## Happiness in the Eyes of the World

I could not have told it better than Ramkrishna Paramahansa does in this beautiful conversation with Swami Vivekanand.

Worry *has* become our way of living. I'll bet you worry from the moment you open your eyes until you close them when you go to sleep. In fact, that worry might make it impossible for you to fall asleep.

Yet your worry is not ill-founded. There is a reason for you to constantly worry. The world we live in has created a perfect environment for us to worry, because, unfortunately, rushing, pushing harder and faster to get the things we have been told will make us happy, has become the motto of the world we live in.

We live in a world where having has taken the place of being.

Based in this belief, we have created a society that supports a never-ending Hamster on a Wheel model of behavior. So, we spend our days working really hard, giving up our time and health in the process, so we can get the things we have been told will make us happy. Unfortunately, when we finally get to that place or get that house, that body, or that relationship, we find that the happiness we experience is short-lived. And once again, we begin our search for the next thing that we believe might make us happy. The constant search for happiness causes us a lot of anxiety, and not achieving that happiness is what causes us to become worn out, frustrated, and depressed. Yet the things we are told will make us happy never end up making us happy for good, and we keep going, like a horse whose owner is using a stick with a carrot on it to make it walk, so do we tiredly keep on stressing ourselves to the bone while the sweet nectar of the carrot named "Lasting Happiness" is never achieved.

## Why do we want to achieve it?

As sentient beings, we all want to be happy and avoid suffering. From plants who turn their leaves to the sun, to our pets, to insects, sentient beings base all of our decisions on the principle of happiness and pain, looking for ways to be happy and avoid the things we believe cause our suffering.

Unfortunately, we have mistaken gratification for real, true happiness and search for it by looking to satisfy our five senses and their desires.

This leads us to behave in ways that will eventually cause us more suffering in the long term. So we end up always chasing happiness, like addicts looking for their next fix, in all the wrong places.

Let's say you are in the middle of traffic, going from home to a job you are not super excited about. A job where you work for over forty hours a week and that, although it gives you a comfortable living, doesn't give you real purpose or meaning. In fact, you hate that this job takes all of your time, so much so that you do not have time to do the things you love, nor to enjoy all the things you are working so hard for. In fact, day in and day out, just like a zombie, you live your life in a state of numbness. In order to get yourself out of this numbness you look for that which in the short-term seems to get you out of that "blah" state, that emptiness. That could be a new gadget like a new luxury car, a bigger home, nicer, more expensive clothes, or a relationship.

To a point, these things will give you some happiness in the short-term – the excitement of getting into a beautiful, fast machine, the sense of accomplishment when getting to buy a new house, the instant confidence a beautiful couture dress can give, or the instant release of oxytocin that a new romantic relationship can activate in the body.

Unfortunately, after some time the new car becomes your ordinary way of transportation, your new house becomes your ordinary house, your new dress becomes your old dress, and the new exciting relationship becomes not so new nor so exciting. And once again you will come to the same state of unhappiness you had before. Once again that piercing feeling of emptiness will slowly come back up, and once again you will search for it somewhere outside of yourself.

Let's say food. How many people, and even kids, nowadays are obese? The reason for this is exactly the same reason we look to have sex or experiment with drugs. All these things will cause the same reaction in your brain. A quick rush of oxytocin, the "love hormone," will shoot out of your brain and all of a sudden you will feel happy. But after that, we will eat more and more in order to keep this feeling coming, usually eating things that can create the feeling faster, like sugar. Similarly, we will fall into having sex before establishing a relationship or use sex as connection when in the wrong relationship because it is, just like food or drugs, a way to escape our reality.

## Why This Turns into Pain, Physically and Emotionally

The reason this turns into pain is because none of these things are going to give you lasting peace. Their very nature is impermanent and one that changes. The new will become old. The most glorious food will be transformed into waste after passing through your digestive system. And the most exciting sex will become regular sex. If you make sex, food, or things your fix to find happiness, you will do ANYTHING to get it and this in its own will cause you suffering.

You will work yourself to the bone, ignoring your health so you can pay for all these things you just have to have in order to be happy.

If you attach your happiness to food, you will eat yourself to obesity or become obsessed with food, and this obsession will not leave you alone and will cause you anxiety. If you become attached to your body you will suffer tremendously when you lose or gain weight, or when you grow old and are close to death, which is the very nature of life. You will spend countless hours and money in order to groom your body, clothe it, and avoid getting old, plus you will attach your sense of self-worth to it. The moment that any change in your physical appearance happens, it will cause tremendous suffering to you.

If you have an attachment to sex, this obsession might destroy good relationships, for you will be looking to have it with different people and at any opportunity. This exposes you to a whole host of diseases that also could cause you even more suffering, or it might keep you attached to the wrong relationship where you might not be appreciated for who you are.

If your happiness is based on being in a relationship, the moment that relationship becomes shaky you will feel completely scared. You will constantly feel jealousy, for anyone is a threat. This can be hell on earth and can become THE reason why you end up losing the very thing you were scared to lose in the first place. This can make life a living hell.

Let's say that you have never been alone, so being in a relationship seems like safety. Your fear of being alone or fear of not finding someone else might keep you prisoner in a stale, unhappy, and sometimes even abusive relationship.

There are many many more examples like this: attachments to money, to status, to titles, to image... to our ego.

So, as you can see, our attachments and our fear of losing them or not having them is what causes our permanent stress and anxiety and, in the long run, is what costs us our sense of lasting joy.

## The Reason for Our Suffering is Called Ignorance

Ignorance means that we are not aware that our attachments are the ones that are causing our own pain. So, we keep doing what we have been doing without realizing that this will only create the same results. In fact, take a moment right now and try to see what is causing you to feel anxious, stressed, or even depressed. When you go to the root of it, you will find an attachment and fear of losing or not getting it.

Yoda from Star Wars said it best:

*"Fear is the path to the dark side. Fear leads to anger. Anger leads to hate. Hate leads to suffering."*

– Yoda

Now in order to dispel darkness we need Light, the Light of Awareness in this case, to get rid of our ignorance. Only Light can dispel darkness.

In order to change anything, we need to become aware of our specific problem. We can't find a solution unless we find a problem to resolve first.

It is only through awareness that we can slowly start making small changes that will have a lasting effect on our lives.

## Exercise 1:

To become aware of what attachments/problems in your own life are causing you the most pain, get yourself a journal and start writing down daily what specific problems you were anxious about.

Be as specific as possible. This will point you to where your fear is and where your inner work is most needed.

If you can, try to pinpoint what that fear is.

**Examples:**

- I am constantly anxious about how I look.
- "I am afraid that I am not lovable enough."
- I am anxious about my next birthday.
- "I am afraid that my biological clock is ticking."
- I am constantly anxious before going to work.
- "I am afraid of realizing that after ten years I will need to look for a new career."

After writing out your anxieties, answer the following questions:

- What are the things you have done to be happy?
- Have they made you happy?
- If yes, for how long, and what happened then?
- If no, what happened?
- Can you pinpoint the attachment or fear that stopped and cut short or denied that happiness?

## Client Success Story

Anette came to me complaining of terrible migraines. These migraines would start every day in the morning and last the whole day. She was at her wits end. She had gone to her MD, who tried everything and finally decided to send her to a neurologist.

He prescribed really strong medication, which didn't help and was causing her extreme fatigue and stomach problems. Anette decided to stop the medication and came to me as her last resort. As I did her medical history intake, where I ask a bunch of questions, she mentioned that her menses had not come for six months and wondered if that might have something to do with her migraines. See, instinctively we know where some of our imbalances might be. We kept talking and I discovered that her work, where she had been for six years now, was causing her a lot of anxiety. She did like what she did – in fact, she loved it and had been doing it on her own with a small group of clients before. But six years ago, her husband was in transition and they needed a steady pay and health insurance, so she decided to take her job at her current company. Six years later she was still there, and she mentioned that she really didn't like to be sitting in front of a desk under white fluorescent light from 8 a.m. to 5 p.m. I asked her why she was still there, since her husband now had a steady job and had gotten good insurance coverage for them both. She said, "I don't know...."

See, the stress and anxiety of having to go to a place she did not enjoy for six years had been causing adrenal fatigue, which in turn had been messing with her hormones to the point of not having regular periods and horrible migraines. Isn't it funny that her migraines would only come up in the morning just as she woke up, right before she had to go to work?

Once we started working together, she became aware how much anxiety this job was truly causing her and the toll it was having on her health. She was not ready to jump back on her own yet, so she decided to talk to her boss and ask to be able to work a couple of days at home and, when at work, to have a couple of breaks where she could go outside, stretch out, and be in nature.

After nine weeks of working together balancing her hormones and establishing the right lifestyle changes, Anette's period came back again, the migraines stopped, and her continuous anxiety about going to work disappeared.

After six months, Anette is still doing great, working half time now, and preparing to get pregnant.

Would balancing her hormones alone have helped? Absolutely. Yet becoming aware of the true root of her problem, which was her anxiety and the depletion caused by her work situation, was the key to not having her migraines come back again.

# CHAPTER FIVE

## SECRET TWO – "ACCEPTANCE AND SELF-LOVE"

*"For God has not given us the spirit of fear; but of power, and of love, and of a sound mind."*

– 2 TIMOTHY 1:7, *THE BIBLE*

### Chronic Anxiety = Chronic Fear

What is chronic anxiety? Chronic anxiety is basically fear, constant fear.

Like I mentioned in the last chapter, chronic anxiety is you being afraid of different things, either in the situation you are in (you are in physical danger) or in the situation you have imagined (which can be the possible negative results or scenarios you have created in your mind). Your fear could also be related to your unwillingness to release your expectations of yourself, of others, and/or a particular situation; and the attachment you have created to things, people, and situations. The biggest one is the attachment to your ego (which feeds itself on how people perceive you and your need to receive love and approval from others).

Fear is what keeps you in that job that no longer suits you, in that relationship that is not right, in that unhealthy cycle of physical disease. Fear is what keeps you in a state of lack, of unworthiness, of unhappiness. Fear keeps you stuck.

Anxiety is the result of carrying this fear for too long without taking action to resolve it. If it goes unaddressed for too long, it will end up wreaking havoc on your health and your life. Why? Because it is your internal voice, that one that the Universe sent to remind you of where you need to go to and work through in order to fulfill your life's destiny.

It is the internal compass reminding you that whatever you are feeling anxious about needs attention. Fear is a wonderful thing if you learn how to navigate it. And the only way to navigate it is with unconditional love. It is by jumping in with both feet and tackling it directly. Only then you are able to transcend that fear and live the life you have always wanted to live. It is your doorway to a life of meaning and purpose, the life you were truly destined to live.

Now, anxiety can be experienced as a physical condition. When you are afraid, you either fight or run like hell. This is a built-in survival mechanism that our bodies have to protect us from danger. Imagine yourself as a caveman. When a predator came close to you, you had two options: Option 1: Run like hell and hope he doesn't catch you. Option 2: Go ahead and fight, fight like you have never fought before!

Biologically, at this moment the body shoots out a bunch of adrenaline, a hormone that tells your body to STOP EVERYTHING AND RUN OR FIGHT! Your pupils dilate, your heart races, blood is pumping. Your digestion stops and, if you heard the saber-toothed tiger in the middle of the night, it would make sure that you are awake! Now, isn't your body marvelous? It absolutely does exactly what it needs to protect you.

It is what we call activating the "fight or flight" response, which is the exact opposite of the "rest and digest" response.

When you experience anxiety, you are actually experiencing fear. This is exactly the same reaction you would have if that saber-toothed tiger were chasing you right now. Your fight or flight response is activated, and you experience a rush of adrenaline with all its accompanying signals. The difference is that in old times, if the saber-toothed tiger didn't eat you, you would go back to your regular daily business until your next encounter with the tiger or another predator. This meant that your body had time to regulate and go back to its general balance. Back then our concerns were survival-related and we were so connected to nature and its rhythmic flow that our bodies, like clocks, would dance with her. We fell asleep when the sun went down, we woke up with the rising of the sun. We worked our bodies for our food and ate when hungry.

If you are suffering from chronic anxiety, your saber-toothed tiger is there all the time. This means your fear will wake up with you, masked with the name anxiety. Once fear settles in the body, there is no opportunity for another emotion, like happiness, to be there. And all of your actions will be created from this perspective. This means it will be really hard for you to appreciate and be grateful for all the blessings you might already be experiencing, since all you can see is danger surrounding you.

## Love Is the Opposite of Fear

*"A Course in Miracles says that only love is real: 'The opposite of love is fear, but what is all-encompassing can have no opposite.' When we think with love, we are literally co-creating with God. And when we're not thinking with love, since only love is real, then we're actually not thinking at all. We're hallucinating. And that's what this world is: a mass hallucination, where fear seems more real than love. Fear is an illusion. Our craziness, paranoia, anxiety and trauma are literally all imagined. That is not to say they don't exist for us as human beings. They do. But our fear is not our ultimate reality, and it does not replace the truth of who we really are. Our love, which is our real self, doesn't die, but merely goes underground."*

– Marianne Williamson, *A Return to Love: Reflections on the Principles of "A Course in Miracles"*

Now, we all experience fear, and this fear can be experienced in all situations – and yes, it's not always just in our mind, sometimes the fear is real. Let's say you are put in a situation where you are afraid for your life. Even in this situation, the Light of Love can transform what seems real – your fear – to what is real – LOVE.

A great example of this comes from Viktor E. Frankl, renowned neurologist and psychiatrist from Austria, author of the book *A Man's Search for Meaning*. In his books he explains what he experienced during the Holocaust. As a Jewish descendant, he was separated from his parents and his newly-wed wife, whom he loved dearly. In the concentration camp, he experienced all kinds of torture and was afraid for his life every day. He had nothing to eat, or very little, and was forced to do intense manual labor for hours, many times without rest. Now, we are talking a life and death situation here, so you would think that stress and anxiety are in fact reasonable responses. Yet he was able to transform this fear through the power of LOVE. You see, at the beginning of his time at the camp, the love he had for his wife kept him going. The thought of reuniting with her helped him stand the pain, the cold, the fear. Reuniting with her was what he wanted the most, so escaping was in his plans constantly. However, while he and his friends were trying to find a way to escape, he was requested to work helping the sick. He started to feel a different type of love, a love that transcends sex and form, a love that aligns us most to the Unconditional Love we come from. His fear disappeared and he started to look forward to the days spent nursing the sick and comforting the dying.

Later, the perfect opportunity arose for him and his friends to escape. Although he didn't know if his wife was dead or alive, it was the perfect time to leave, to escape the suffering, the anxiety, the fear... but amazingly, he chose not to. Unconditional Love had won, and he could not see himself anywhere else. See, since he couldn't change the situation, he decided to change himself, and he was transformed by this love.

This Unconditional Love we come from – this love which is the only real thing, the only Truth, the only unchangeable, ever present, never changing reality – is what we are and what we come from. Where Love exists, Fear cannot be. Try it! Think about someone you love the most, picture them clearly in your mind's eye, let the love you have for them expand all over your being. Now try, as you are holding this image of Love in your mind and in your being, to be anxious, afraid. See? It is impossible. Just like Light is to Darkness, Love and Fear cannot exist at the same time. Love is the only Truth.

Everything else is an illusion, the illusion of the collective consciousness we have infected each other with. But when you awaken to this love, this love that is already in you as YOU, then all the suffering disappears, all the fear disappears, for you see life as it is, not as you imagined it to be.

Even the direst of situations gives you an opportunity to be more aligned to that Love that you came from.

## Self-Love vs Ego

One way you can start returning to Love is by giving YOURSELF unconditional Self-Love first. Why is this so important? Because we cannot give what we do not have.

If we do not know how to love ourselves, how to take care of ourselves and nurture ourselves, then, my darling, how can you give and take care of others? When you start practicing Self-Love, what you are truly doing is taking away the layers of hate, judgment, self-doubt, narrow-mindedness, anger, fear, jealousy, resentment, pettiness, greed, separation, etc. that keep you from the Love and Happiness you already are. Like a diamond hidden in a piece of coal, by slowly polishing it through the fire of purification you will slowly rediscover the Love and Happiness you are so anxious and stressed to find.

Once again, the Light of Awareness can start the transformation, which is looking at where the problem begins. And it begins by understanding the difference between Self-Love and ego. Ego is the opposite of Self-Love. Ego is the one that tells you, "ME first!" without regards to anyone else. I, I, I. This is the one that seeks separation, that does not understand that we are all connected or that by hurting others in the short-term to have your own satisfaction taken care of, you will in the end cause yourself more suffering.

I give you an example:

Let's say you work in an advertising agency and you are in charge of a team. You and the team are responsible for coming up with brilliant ideas that will be bought by your clients and could eventually win awards.

Now, if you work with your ego, you will always want to prove that your ideas are the best, and you will always want to present your ideas. You will be unaware of the frustration that will create in your team. They will no longer even try to give you ideas; the spark of creativity will be drained and soon enough they will be looking for a new place to work.

Now, even if you are a creative genius, you will have times where you are not that creative and you still will have to create. Wouldn't it be great if an amazing idea were still presented, even if it wasn't yours? Wouldn't it be sad if, because of your own ego, you hadn't given the opportunity to other creative geniuses to shine as well? Wouldn't it suck to lose really amazing talent just because you needed to show that YOU are the best?

All these last results will have an impact on your life – a negative impact, by the way. And if you look more deeply, you will realize that your desire to SHINE, to be number ONE, to be recognized and to be right, is a deep desire for APPROVAL AND LOVE from others. Why? Because you haven't been able to give this to yourself. You still think that your value comes from outside recognition, be it your trophies, your wins, your clothes, your things, your success, your looks, your... (INSERT WHATEVER THING THAT IT IS NOT YOU). You are love itself, you are ENOUGH.

You, your true being, not your things, not your body, not the opinions of others, not even your thoughts. YOU, the Soul, the eternal LOVE, the silent observer of the play that constantly flows.

YOU, who come from Unconditional Love, and ARE Unconditional LOVE.

## Developing Unconditional Self-Love and a New Dream

Developing unconditional Self-Love is not something we need to learn. Quite the opposite, in fact. What we need to learn is how to unlearn all the things that keep us from being connected to the unconditional Self-Love we already have. We need to become aware of all the stories that we keep telling ourselves in order to stay stuck in the same place. Stories like: "It's too hard," "I don't have time," "I don't have the resources," "I have tried everything, and nothing works," "It is not that bad," "It's not me, it's my situation," "It's because of my parents, my boss, my spouse, my kids, my (insert anything other than yourself)." Developing Self-Love is developing an unbreakable determination that you are a priority. You are worth investing in. You are the architect of your own destiny. Nobody else, nothing else.

All these stories you keep telling yourself are the ways your brain and your ego work. If you reconnect with Love, your ego doesn't have anywhere to live anymore, and your brain is basically reacting to the number one fear out there: FEAR OF CHANGE. Yet fear of change is what keeps you where you are: stuck, unhappy, stressed, anxious, and depressed.

Fear of change is what keeps you from creating the life you always imagined. Fear of change will keep you stuck, unhappy, and afraid.

Fear is the opposite of love. Fear is where your wounds are. But you can heal yourself. You can access the power that already lives within you and create a new reality, create a new dream. A dream where you feel the love and recognition and validation you have been craving since you were a little child, but which is not attached to anything or anyone outside yourself. A dream where you discover the beauty and the magic that already lives within you.

Michelangelo, the great artist, was asked how he had created David from one piece of marble, to which he replied, "David was always there in the marble. I just took away everything that was not David."

So too, my darling, the masterpiece that is you is already there. We just need to carve out the rest.

## Exercise 1: A Contract between Your Most Loving True Self and Yourself

Congratulations.

You just made an exceptional commitment to yourself and your future.

What you put in, you will get out. Please read and sign the following:

*Dearest (WRITE YOUR NAME HERE),*

*After careful thought and consideration, I hereby promise:*

*To honor my body as the temple of my Soul*

*To offer it healthy foods and drinks*

*To realize that I deserve to be healthy and happy*

*To forgive mySelf*

*To cherish mySelf*

*To keep going through the changes that will destroy my ego even if they feel uncomfortable*

*To love mySelf unconditionally to face the fears that bind me*

*To overcome the addictions that hurt me*

*To love and appreciate myself for what who I am*

*To accept that I have the power to heal myself*

*To accept myself and be grateful for me just the way I am*

*To listen to the messages my body is sending me when I am tired, hurt, or sick*

*To understand that my unexpressed emotions and thoughts affect me and affect my body*

*(List additional promises)*

*I love you so much,*

*(Please sign here)*

## Exercise 2: Self-Love and Compassion Meditation

Every day for twenty-one days, start and end your day with this meditation.

Find a quiet space where you can sit without being disturbed. Sit on a chair or the floor with your legs closed (only if this is comfortable to you). Make sure your spine is straight and that you are not resting your back on the chair.

If you are sitting on a chair, allow your feet to press firmly on the ground and your palms to rest gently on your thighs. No straining.

Now gently close your eyes and start focusing on your breath without trying to control it or judge it, just breathing in and out.

If any thought comes to your mind, allow it to come and go. Once you feel a bit more settled in your breath, you will repeat the following words. Do it aloud first. It is great to hear yourself say this to yourself out loud. Once it feels rooted in your mind, you can keep saying it silently in your mind only.

*"May I be happy.*

*May I be peaceful.*

*May I have ease of well-being.*

*May I live in harmony and Grace.*

*May I love and be loved.*

*May I be free from suffering."*

Allow this wonderful prayer to resonate in the core of your being and watch the amazing transformation it will have in your life.

## Exercise 3: Mirror Talk

Looking deeply into your eyes in the mirror and say: I love you.

I am enough.

I deserve to be happy.

At the beginning it might feel odd to you to say such things, but with time you will start feeling more and more comfortable and feeling it deep in your body.

Do this practice consistently for twenty-one days.

## Client Success Story

I will let Any (a patient of mine when I had one of my centers in Guatemala) tell her story in her own words and with her permission. She has a very popular blog for moms in Guatemala, and this is what she wrote:

*I've been wanting to write this article for a few weeks and I always found an excuse not to do it. It is not because it is something negative, but rather because it means something SO profound in my life that I do not know how to summarize it so that you do not get bored with reading a long testament. But here goes... my experience with Dr. Michelle Eggenberger, that changed my life.*

*Two months ago, I got serious pain, real serious pain in my back. I stopped at the emergency room at the hospital because the pain was unbearable. The diagnosis was terrible: scoliosis (deviated column), four hernias, compressed discs, compressed nerves, a muscle spasm... in short, everything that could go wrong with my back, I had it! The neurosurgeon told me that I could not have surgery and that basically everything that could be done was pain management and physical therapy. He gave me some medicines that left me knocked out for more than two weeks and after that I refused to continue with them. So, I looked for another option that sounded more interesting: ACUPUNCTURE.*

*My sister-in-law came across a Dharma Center video on Facebook (now Dharma Clinic/ Lake Mary) and when I saw it, I knew that that was what I was looking for. Upon entering the clinic, the first thing I saw were more than fifteen diplomas in all kinds of alternative healing from Dr. Eggenberger, and I admit that gave me peace of mind. I came to the free half-hour appointment where they explained to me what the treatment consists of, and its cost. And with that little decision I began my path to healing, not only in body, but surprisingly in mind and Soul as well.*

*I laid on my stomach, dying of fear thinking about the needles, but when the doctor started to put them on I realized that honestly, they do not hurt. Even though my problem was in the lower back, when she was working on the middle of my back, all of a sudden there was a special point that hurt terribly. I even jumped! But the strangest thing of all was that it felt like something deep inside me got moved and a river of tears and accumulated sadness started to pour out. I cried and cried during the whole session, not from physical pain because of the needle, but of sadness! The doctor explained that at the points where I felt most pain, it was because there was blocked energy and depending on the location, that was its meaning. These blockages are mainly emotions or thoughts that we haven't dealt with and that at the end cause us harm from the Spiritual level until they reach the physical and that is why disease arises.*

*It was the only session where I cried. From then on, I only felt relief. Each session I went to, the doctor helped me find the emotional reasons for my back pain. It was an emotional and physical therapy that I was experiencing, but mainly it was a revolution in the way I looked at my body and healing.*

*My last appointment arrived, and I felt real regret that I had finished the treatment. Having recovered the mobility and functionality in the physical was only one of the benefits. The changes I had made in my body and in my Soul had been so profound that I am sure that they will accompany me all my life.*

*I said goodbye to the doctor with a very strong hug. I can honestly say that in those sessions I became very fond of her. The love that she puts into her work, in knowing you deeply and genuinely worrying about the holistic well-being of her patients, is hard to find these days. I have no words to thank the Universe for putting me on the path to Dr. Eggenberger, and I recommend her with closed eyes for anyone who wishes to heal in a truly profound way.*

Any was a great patient. As we worked together, she was courageous enough to see where her wounds were, where she needed to heal from the deepest level, and where she had stopped taking care of herself and showing herself unconditional love and kindness. This allowed for her to realign her body, her mind, and her Soul and start her true process of complete healing and deep transformation!

# CHAPTER SIX

## SECRET THREE – "GENERATING ENERGY"

*"In the past, people practiced the Tao, the Way of Life. They understood the principle of balance as represented by the transformations of the energies of the universe. They formulated exercises to promote energy flow to harmonize themselves with the universe. They ate a balanced diet at regular times, arose and retired at regular hours, avoided over stressing their bodies and minds, and refrained from overindulgence of all kinds. They maintained well-being of body and mind; thus, it is not surprising that they lived over one hundred years."*

– Excerpt from Nei Jing, translated by Maoshing Ni

In this chapter, you will learn basic concepts of Traditional Chinese Medicine to help you understand the holistic approach to your body. This magical and sacred medicine has been around for thousands of years, and to explain and really understand its concepts needs deep study. Here you will find a very gentle introduction to basic concepts like the Five Elements and Qi, to make the concepts accessible and easy to understand. I'll also provide specific recommendations about food, lifestyle, and alternative therapies that I have found have incredible transformative effects, not only in the body but the mind and the Soul.

## The Body as Part of Nature

When you see a flower, what do you see? Do you see just a flower? Now, again this time, put the book down for a moment, close your eyes, and picture the flower as clearly as you can...

What did you see? Could you see the clouds full of precious rain that watered her?

Could you see and feel the earth full of minerals, a nourishment that fed her as she was just a seedling?

Could you feel the warmth of the sun that helped her grow and the wind that gently rocked her, so she could show off her glow?

In every petal, in her sweet fragrance, the whole Universe is present and so she too is part of it all and moves with the ebbs and the flows of nature's energy.

Every cell in our bodies also contains the whole Universe in it; therefore, we are also governed by its rhythmic nature.

Just like this excerpt of the Nei Jing explains, the secret to living a long healthy life is to be in harmony with the Universe. Allowing ourselves and our bodies to dance with the ebbs and flows of the ever-changing yet constant energy of the Universe. What do I mean? Well, I mean we are all part of this beautiful dance, our bodies are in direct contact with the natural energy. To the point that in ancient times women's cycles were so aligned with the lunar cycles that the crops would be sown, plowed, and harvested according to them. Nowadays we have lost our contact to nature and in turn to the basic rhythms of the Universe. This misalignment is what causes disease in the body, the mind, and the Spirit.

Our foods are no longer pure and simple. We have managed to contaminate our foods with pesticides, antibiotics, and steroids. We no longer take it from the earth, but from huge manufacturers whose goal is to mass produce no matter what the cost, to the earth, to the animals we consume, and to the people themselves. Greed has become the name of the game. Unfortunately for us, we have no time to reflect on this. We are constantly rushed from here to there, so we eat the easy fast foods loaded with preservatives and chemicals, and we call food that can stay exactly the same for over thirty days "a hamburger." By the way, if your food has a longer shelf life than you do, that is a pretty good sign that what you are eating is not food!

We eat at our desks, if we eat at all, load ourselves with carbs, sugars, and caffeine, to help a body that can no longer go, keep up. Loaded with caffeine, sugar, and adrenaline from the constant stress and anxiety, we can't sleep, turning, tossing in bed. Exhausted but with a racing mind. So, we numb ourselves with food and TV until we finally succumb and start taking sleeping pills or alcohol to help us relax and fall asleep. Unfortunately, even medicated or passed out, we have no restful sleep. No wonder we wake up exhausted! And the lack of sleep can further create havoc and depletion in the body until it also starts affecting the mind. No wonder they kept prisoners awake for days as a form of torture. If you ever have suffered from insomnia or had to constantly feed a crying baby, you know that's true!

So again, we start the cycle the next day: caffeine to wake up, a rushed breakfast (if any, and usually high in carbs and sugar) to get us going. Once the sugar high crashes, usually at mid-morning, we have another form of caffeine, maybe a soda, then again a fast food lunch, then a late, unhealthy dinner that makes it hard for to digestion to rest. This late, unhealthy dinner will in turn give you acid reflux or GERD, exacerbated by the fact that it will no longer allow you to sleep, which will make it necessary for you to take both medication for sleeping and now for acid reflux or GERD, too, which in turn has another myriad side effects like inappropriate food absorption, which can lead to a leaky gut, which in turn will cause all the toxins to leak back into the body, opening the door to conditions like fibro-myalgia, lupus, chronic fatigue disorder, all autoimmune diseases, and cancer. Phew! Just writing that made me feel overwhelmed! With all that in mind, take a little breather and time to reflect...

Isn't it interesting that the farther away we are from nature and its natural flow, the more these conditions are becoming the norm, when not so long ago they were rarely heard of?

This is only one example among many of how far from nature we have become, and how this slowly eats away at our health and our peace of mind.

Like crazy rats in laboratories, we run and run on the wheel, fed with sugar-infused water, without stopping and thinking that we, unlike rats, have the capacity and freedom to stop. Until we do!

# The Five Elements and Their Constitutional Type

*"Nature does not hurry, yet everything is accomplished."*

– Lao Tzu

Traditional Chinese Medicine is based on the Principals of the Tao. It is the balance of energies, which are opposite in nature (e.g. dark and light, hot and cold, masculine and feminine) and constantly interact with each other, creating and opposing each other infinitely. The night will give rise to the morning and so the morning will once again give rise to the night. So the cycles of energy move, and within them the Five Elements, which also promote, control, contract, and give rise to each other.

Once more this eternal dance of nature that, as Lao Tzu mentions, doesn't hurry yet accomplishes everything, lives in and influences our body and mind too.

All the functions of the body are divided into systems that are represented by an element. Your physical and mental constitution are also governed by elements. This can make you prone to certain challenges physically, mentally, and spiritually as well. Understanding each of the elements and how your constitutional element works can give you insight into what to do to avoid getting sick.

These Five Elements in our body are Water, Wood, Fire, Earth, and Metal. Each element rules a particular system in the body. It represents a yin or yang organ and its functions in the body. It manifests in a particular tissue, it has a color, a smell, and a taste and these characteristics will give us insight into the particular imbalance in the body. Let's take for example the element Water.

## *WATER*

*The Water sign rules the kidneys and the bladder.*

*It is represented as the season of winter and its emotion is fear.*

*Its sense organ is the ears, and it manifests in the hair and the scalp.*

*Its body fluid is urine and its climate sensitivity is cold.*

*Its smell is putrid, and its taste is salty.*

*It rules the bones.*

What?! LOL! I know. I know when you read it like this it makes absolutely no sense, nor do I expect for you to understand while reading this book what took me four years to learn and many, many more to properly apply.

So, let me give you a little insight: the Water element represents the kidneys and the bladder, which means that it governs everything that has to do with water and fluid transformation in the body, like your urine, sperm, retention of water, etc. Winter is the season that represents Water, so in winter if you have any deficiencies in this element you can expect to see more of them. All the elements and organs have an emotion that represents them and Water's emotion is fear, so too much fear depletes the kidneys and the bladder. That is why little kids, whose kidney and bladder system is not fully developed yet, might soil themselves when scared. Also, a deficiency in the kidney and bladder system can cause you to feel afraid all the time.

The kidney and bladder system are also in charge of sperm and fertility, and any issue related to this system can create fertility problems in the long run.

One thing we learn as physicians as part of our diagnostic methods is to see, smell, and, in some cases, even taste. (Well, that happened in old times, when physicians tasted urine for example to see if it was sweet for possible diabetes – thankfully we have technology now!) This can give us further clues to a person's condition. Putrid is the smell we can smell if a person has a condition related to the Water element.

The Water element rules the bones, so any problem with the bones – fragile bones, bone fractures, osteoporosis, osteopenia etc. – is directly related to this element and system. We will look at this element and if it's in balance in order to rectify these conditions.

Its sense organs are the ears and it manifests in the scalp and hair. So, when a person has hearing difficulties, problems with tinnitus, etc., we know to look at this system. Also, any hair loss or scalp problem can have a direct relationship to the Water element.

Here are a few physical problems that denote that the Water element is out of balance: hypersensitive/dulled vision and hearing; ringing in the ears; headaches above the eyes and vortex; hardening of blood vessels and cartilages; rigidity of joints and muscles; weak and stiff spine, lower body, and joints; degeneration of disks; osteoporosis; frequent urination; kidney and bladder stones; prematurely gray, thin hair; wrinkled skin; infertility; frigidity; impotence; and hypertension.

In this section, I will outline the characteristics of the other four systems with their representations. This can give you a new perspective on seeing your pains and ailments and a new hope, knowing that just a tiny imbalance in these can create a difference in the whole body. Take the principles of what I explained about the Water element and apply them to each element.

## *WOOD*

*Organs: Liver and Gallbladder*

*Emotion: Anger*

*Season: Spring*

*Manifests: Nails*

*Body Fluid: Tears*

*Climate Sensitivity: Wind*

*Smell: Rancid*

*Taste: Sour*

Common conditions: high blood/labile blood pressure; oily skin/hair; boils; cramps of long muscles, hands, or feet; vertigo; ringing ears; constipation with cramps; spasms; sciatica; pain in ribs; heartburn; difficulty swallowing; eye/ear pain; breast pain; tendon injuries; hypoglycemia;

sensitivity to light or sound; cystitis; urethritis; tendonitis; lax joints and tense muscles; irritable colon; chronic pain in the neck and bones; painful menses; PMS.

## *FIRE*

*Organs: Heart and Small Intestine*

*Emotion: Joy*

*Season: Summer*

*Manifests: Complexion*

*Body Fluid: Sweat*

*Climate Sensitivity: Heat*

*Smell: Scorched*

*Taste: Bitter*

Common conditions: enlarged heart; profuse/frequent perspiration; flushed face; irregular/ rapid heartbeat; chest pain; strong erratic or slow irregular pulse; overheats easily; weak heart; sores of the mouth, tongue, or lips; pulmonary hypertension; dry, painful eczema; easy sexual excitement but difficult to please; low blood pressure; faints or gets dizzy easily; pale with flushed cheeks; tires easily from excitement; cannot sustain sexual excitement; premature orgasm.

## *EARTH*

*Organs: Spleen and Stomach*

*Emotion: Overthinking*

*Season: Late Summer*

*Manifests: Lips*

*Body Fluid: Saliva*

*Climate Sensitivity: Dampness*

*Smell: Fragrant*

*Taste: Sweet*

Common conditions: excess appetite; water retention; irregular bowel movements and urination; difficulty with weight management; digestive disorders; metabolic, muscle, and lymphatic dysfunction; venous disorders; sticky saliva and perspiration; PMS with lethargy; aching and swelling, sticky, puffy eyelids; heavy aching head and eyes.

## METAL

*Organs: Lungs and Large Intestine*

*Emotion: Grief*

*Season: Winter*

*Manifests: Skin, Body and Hair*

*Body Fluid: Mucus*

*Climate Sensitivity: Dryness*

*Smell: Rotten*

*Taste: Pungent*

Common conditions: respiratory disorders; skin ailments; dehydration; over-expanded chest; dry cough with tight chest; sinus headache; stress incontinence; congested nose, throat, and sinus; headaches from sadness and disappointment; varicose veins; sneeze or cough with changes in temperature and humidity.

When we use the Five Element Theory, we no longer see the body as separate parts but a whole eco-cosmos that needs to be balanced for all of its parts to work well.

Let me give you an example:

Let's say you have a beautiful, green tree. All of a sudden, some leaves on a branch start getting brown, drying up. So, in the conventional medicine approach, a physician comes and treats it with some type of medicine that maybe combats the bug or plague he thinks is causing the browning of the leaves. It might also add a green coloring (a.k.a. your pharmaceuticals) so you no longer see the brown. Now you are happy, your tree looks green and beautiful, and you go on.

A couple of months later the color starts coming off and the brown has appeared again in the old leaves – but not only that, now more leaves seem to be brown. The whole branch now seems to be covered by them. Our conventional medicine approach might be, well, let's just cut off the branch so it won't infect the others. So once again now, without the sick branch, your tree seems green again and all is well – until it is not. Months have passed and now more brown leaves are appearing again, but now on different branches.

This is very similar to our approach to disease. We believe that each part of our body is different and we focus on the symptoms but rarely go beyond that.

Following the tree example, here is an example of how a Traditional Chinese Medicine (TCM) physician would assess the situation

A TCM physician will look at the leaves, but will also look at the whole tree. She will see if there is enough or too much sun on your tree, she will make sure the tree has the right amount of water. She will check the earth to make sure that there are enough nutrients for the tree. Are the roots healthy? How do all the other branches look? After all this, the TCM physician realizes that the fertilizer you have been using has an additive that is damaging the root of the tree. She will recommend an organic, additive-free fertilizer, plus she will show you how to check if the condition will reappear, will reinforce the natural properties of the tree, and will treat the initial tree with the sap of another tree to promote healing.

In general, she will make sure that all the elements are working correctly so your tree not only does not get sick again but also so it can flourish!

This is a very superficial view of the Five Elements, like staring at the tip of an iceberg. But it can hopefully open your mind to a new way of seeing your body, mind, and emotions and help you realize that there are other ways of healing. In fact, like life itself, your body pulsates with the very energy of life and only needs the right environment to heal. If you are enjoying this approach, you can go to **www.theenergeticsofjoy.com/elementquiz** and there you will get a better idea of what your constitution is, what element you need to balance, and how! If you would like to work on your specific case, I am always available to offer you guidance to get your body into alignment; again, you can send me an email at **info@theenergeticsofjoy.com**.

## Qi (Vital Energy) and the Energetics of the Body and the Mind

*"That which animates life is called Qi (chee). The concept of Qi is absolutely at the heart of Chinese Medicine. Life is defined by Qi even though is impossible to grasp, measure, quantify, see or isolate. Immaterial yet essential, the material world is formed by it. Matter is Qi taking shape."*

– Harriet Seinfeld, L.AC. and Efram Korngold, L.AC., O.M.D., *Between Heaven and Earth*

Qi, the vital energy, permeates every single atom of everything created. It cannot be seen or explained, yet it exists. Quantum physics is finally catching on to this concept, yet there is so much further to go.

Qi, the vital energy or life force, is what animates the body and its functions. In order for health to exist, there has to be enough Qi (pronounced "chee") in the body and this Qi needs to flow freely.

Once this Qi has become stagnant for a while, disease appears in the body.

There are different types of Qi, from the denser, like the physical body, to the more sublime, like the breath, and even further, our thoughts.

Many practices have been created in order to cultivate this Qi and keep it flowing properly, practices like Qi Gong, Tai Chi, Acupuncture, Yoga, Pranayama, etc.

Why? Because, as I mentioned before, if the Qi becomes deficient or stagnant it will open the door to disease. Easy ways to know if your Qi is deficient or stagnant without deep study include: feeling fatigued most of the time, especially after eating; having irregular menstrual cycles;

sighing a lot; feeling forgetful; having muscular tension, especially in the neck and back; or feeling easily irritable, angry, and emotional. However, in general terms, if you have *any* pathologic physical or emotional manifestation, your Qi is not flowing properly.

Taxing the body with excessive physical stress, too much food, the wrong food, alcohol, not enough exercise, or not enough relaxation will cause the Qi of the body to become deficient or stagnant. Taxing the mind with too much anxiety, overthinking, anger, fear, or sadness will also eventually deplete the Qi and cause it to stagnate.

In order to keep the right amount of Qi in your body and make sure it flows appropriately, you need to be aware of your thoughts, eat the right foods in the right quantities, give yourself plenty of time to rest and relax, exercise your body, and practice peace.

## Food

Food is very important in the creation of Qi and the cultivation of it.

Just like the body, Qi permeates all food that we eat and gives it qualities that we will absorb when we eat it. For example, leafy greens like kale, spinach, and arugula, and fresh organic vegetables are bursting with Qi. The minute the body absorbs them, the body takes those qualities, and you will feel vibrant and alive, your mental state will be clear, and your emotions will be balanced.

Foods that are dead, greasy, or fried will make you feel dead, greasy, and fried.

The concept of "we are what we eat" is literally true, and learning about the energetics of your food will help you not only create more energy and vibrancy in the body, but can be used to achieve higher levels of consciousness, too, if done appropriately.

Avoid overcooked and reheated food. Stay away from food that has too many preservatives and, if you can, try to avoid animal products as much as possible, especially if you do not know where they are coming from.

To the Earth element ruled by the stomach and the spleen system, which rules metabolism and transportation and transformation of food and fluids, anything cold will eventually damage it, so try to lightly cook your vegetables – you can even gently pass your salad through boiling water, so it is pre-cooked. Dairy and sugars are phlegm-forming in the body, which creates stasis of Qi and will make you feel heavy and drained, so eat as little as possible of them.

Avoid caffeine and sugars, as they are sure stimulants to the brain. That includes white pasta, rice, or any simple carbohydrate that will transform into sugar quickly and cause havoc in your nervous system.

The same stress and fear that produces adrenaline in our bodies will create the same in a dying animal, especially if it has been suffering for a long time, so becoming vegetarian is a great way of raising your energy. However, it is very important that you know how to become vegetarian safely and are guided by a professional, so you do not create any more deficiencies in the body. Now, I know this is not for everyone, so if you cannot become vegetarian all the time at least try to join the movement Meat Free Mondays. Your body, the planet, and thousands of innocent little lives will benefit.

Add germinated seeds to your plate as often as you can. Sprouted almonds, for example, are bursting with life and protein! The yogic diet is full of amazing secrets about how to stay healthy and young looking – plus if you really want to calm your Spirit and elevate your consciousness, there are great secrets you can learn – but there are way too many to write about in this book. If you are interested in knowing how you can raise your consciousness through food, you will be able to do so in my coming book, *The Energetics of Food*. For now, remember that the right food can bring health to the body while the wrong food can bring sickness to the body. Lots can be learned about the energetics of food. But to start simply, eat fresh, live, and organic and you will be on the right track. One thought that really helps me is, "With this food am I feeding my health, or I am feeding my disease?"

## Acupuncture

Acupuncture, one of the most-used tools of Traditional Chinese Medicine, is a great way to reboot the whole Qi flow in your body. Thin, cat-hair-like needles are inserted in specific points in the body. This points are on the meridians, or energetic pathways, of the body and have an exterior-interior connection with the body. When these needles are manipulated, they create a reaction in the body which balances the Qi, allowing it to flow and increase or decrease based on what the body needs. It reboots the body and balances the neuroendocrine axis, balancing hormones and therefore the chemicals of the brain as well. In choosing the right Acupuncturist, make sure she/he is a Doctor of Oriental Medicine and that she/he has had the training to understand the deeper principles of Traditional Chinese

Medicine. Give it a try – it is truly fascinating to see people start healing when conventional medicine had given them no hope. Plus, if you were wondering, no, the needles don't hurt!

## Yoga

Yoga is a science in itself, the science of self-discovery and Self-Realization, which is the highest goal. To do yoga, you do not need to change religions, nor become a Hindu. Yet yoga and basically the asanas, which are the physical postures, are a great way of getting the Qi or, in yogic terms, prana, of the body moving. Another aspect is Pranayama, or breathing techniques. As I mentioned before, the breath is a subtler type of Qi and learning to control it will help your mind to slow down. Depending on what breathing technique you use, you can create different aspects of Qi in the body and mind.

There are breathing techniques to heat or cool the body, there are breathing techniques to slow down the breath and thus the mind, there are breathing techniques to help digestion, there are breathing techniques to balance the two hemispheres of the brain.

Breathing is one of the key ways to reduce stress and anxiety, and remembering to breathe and learning how to do it correctly can be life-changing! Yet again, let me remind you that although here in the West we perceive yoga as pure exercise, the real yoga, which is based on the yoga sutras of Patanjali, is a whole system whose basis is the Yamas and Niyamas, or ethical rules. Like my beloved teacher Shri Dharma Mittra says, "There is no yoga without the Yamas and Niyamas!"

Just like with acupuncture, finding the right yoga teacher is going to be key to your success. Make sure they properly understand your condition and what you are looking for, and even if you are just looking for the physical benefits, yoga is a great way to align the body and get the Qi/prana flowing correctly!

## Meditation

Erratic Qi disturbs the mind and the body, so learning how to settle it can be one of the most important ways you can learn to not leak energy and keep yourself not only healthy but happy. Meditation is the answer for such a challenging fit. Just like in Pranayama, meditation has many different techniques, from just focus meditation, to analytic meditation, to walking meditation, to... you name it. The simplest way to meditate is by focusing on the breath and trying to stay focused there for as long as you can.

Many people tell me that they can't meditate because their mind won't leave them alone. But what if I tell you that all the thoughts you believe are not letting you meditate are the very thoughts that you are thinking about all the time? By meditating you are only becoming aware of how much your mind truly runs nonstop. Bringing awareness to anything is the first step for change, remember? So, by meditating you start observing your thoughts, what their quality is, if they are positive or negative, and slowly learning to change and hopefully to stop them so you can be present to yourself as the "Eternal Observer," realizing that your thoughts are like mere clouds passing by in a beautiful empty sky. To start, it is not necessary for you to meditate for twenty minutes. You can start with five minutes and then increase your time. Again, guidance is key. Once you have been taught how to create a safe space, what the proper sitting position is, and what the proper alignment of eyes, sight, and tongue placement looks like, you can do it yourself. There are great apps you can use like Insight or Timer.

Give meditation a try and see how settling your mind can give you more clarity, energy, focus, and most importantly, peace!

## Water

The importance of drinking water is hardly ever mentioned. Our bodies are 60–90% water depending on our age, babies are almost all water! So, make sure you are drinking plenty. Not drinking enough water can cause fatigue, brain fog, irritability, headaches, palpitations, anxiety, dehydration, insomnia, problems with digestion, high blood pressure, and more! So make sure you are drinking enough!

## Rest

> *"Relaxation is the best antidote to impurities."*
> – Sri Dharma Mittra

Appropriate rest is essential for true healing. Make sure you rest and allow the body to regenerate and heal. Try going to bed at 10 p.m. and waking at 6:00 a.m. These are the best times for the body to relax and rest.

Make sure to eat at least two hours before going to bed. Allow for your bedroom to be completely dark, and keep electronics away. Also, disconnect from TV and electronics at least one hour before going to sleep.

In general, allowing for your body to become closer to the flow of nature will assure that you stay happy and healthy.

Your body can heal itself, it just needs the right elements to do so!

## Exercise:

- Do the Five Element Quiz at **www.theenergeticsofjoy/ myelementquiz**
- Follow the recommendations based on your element type
- Download the Uyai or Ocean Breath Meditation
- Increase water intake, reduce or eliminate caffeine and sodas, increase your greens and vegetables to an 80–20% ratio (80% greens and veggies, 20% protein and carbs)
- Buy fresh, local and organic
- Go to bed earlier

## Client Success Story

Thomas, a busy professional, had been diagnosed with multiple sclerosis. He came to me because he had started to feel numbness in his feet and had been stumbling and falling. Although he knew the seriousness of his diagnosis, Thomas had the amazing insight of knowing that he could do something about it. As we worked together and he started to feel improvement in his feet and his attitude, Thomas realized the healing power of his own body and felt empowered to learn more. He began learning about foods and their effects on the body. Every time he would come in for an appointment, he would tell me about what he was learning and doing to detox his body and increase his vitamin levels. We would discuss the different aspects of his food, his rest, his exercise, and what other things he could do. In an ocean of doctors who didn't give him lots of hope, I believed in him as much as he started to believe in his own power to transform his health and life in the process. Thomas not only regained full function in his legs, he is one of the healthiest people I know. He became a health coach, a triathlon participant, and even transformed the way he worked to allow for more work-life balance – and surprise, he did even better business-wise and financially.

That is the power of the body, given the right environment, and that is the power of the Spirit when the mind is clear and focused!

# CHAPTER SEVEN

## SECRET FOUR – "IMAGINATION VS REALITY"

*"We are what we think.*
*All that we are arises with our thoughts.*
*With our thoughts we make the world.*
*Speak or act with an impure mind*
*And trouble will follow you*
*As the wheel follows the ox that draws the cart.*
*We are what we think.*
*All that we are arises with our thoughts.*
*With our thoughts we make the world.*

*Speak or act with a pure mind*
*And happiness will follow you*
*As your shadow, unshakable.*"

— TRANSLATED BY THOMAS BYROM, FROM
*THE DHAMMAPADA*

In this chapter we will be exploring your mind and the thoughts that you are entertaining. Your thoughts create your emotions and these emotions are the ones that move you into actions, which become habits, which slowly become your life. In this chapter you will become aware of how your thoughts determine your reality, how some ways of thinking have self-sabotaging, defeating effects while others have the capacity to lift you up and help you create the beautiful life you want and deserve!

## Perception vs Reality

Have you been in love? Or have you had a big crush? I am sure you have. And do you remember how you felt? How everything seemed to be perfect no matter what was going on outside yourself? You were late to work... who cares? He lives in a tiny, dirty apartment with four other roommates, that's fine! They cut the electric power 'cause you didn't pay? Just another reason to light the candles and make it a romantic evening! No matter what was happening, you looked at life with "rose-colored glasses" and life was fine! The same is true for the opposite situation. Let's say you just got dumped. You are heartbroken and nothing goes well. You live in an amazing, beautiful home? Who cares, you are still lonely. You have lost twenty pounds and now you are in your perfect weight? So what, you still feel ugly. You finally got the promotion you were working so hard for? It is all the same to you now....

As you can see, the state of our mind determines our reality. I remember one time as I went back to Guatemala I was walking with my husband along the shore. Beautiful, huge homes surrounded the coast line. In this ideal scene we saw a group of around five kids. They were dressed in rags and had no towels or "nice umbrellas" to speak of. They looked truly out of place on this ritzy beach. Yet what seemed even more out of place were their huge smiles, the joy that they were experiencing as they kept being carried on and off the sand by the waves. Their laughter was contagious and as they saw us approach they invited us to play in the ocean. How could these kids, who obviously didn't have a million-dollar home, nice bathing suits, or even towels to speak of, be so happy? They had a pure mind and were in a state of abundance and gratitude. The houses, the suits, the umbrellas, they were just props! The happiness was radiating from within! Now, I am not telling you that you need to be poor and not have things or let yourself go and not take care of yourself – not at all. What I am saying though is that your experience of life is purely based on your perception of it and that becomes your reality. Ask yourself, if you have a big white wall and right in the middle of it there is a black dot, what do you see? Do you choose to focus on the dot or on the big white wall? It is all up to you, but the reality is that what we focus on grows and what we resist persists! So, with that awareness, do you know what you have been focusing on? Does it contribute to your anxiety and your sense of unhappiness?

## If you are going to assume, assume the best!

As I discussed before, anxiety is basically fear, in this case fear of the scenarios we create based on our assumptions. Our assumptions are not based on reality, they are based on what we think can happen or what we believe people are thinking. Assumptions are imaginary situations that we construct. Unfortunately, most of us are chronically predisposed to assume the worse and act accordingly, even if the situation hasn't presented itself. This makes us act in a certain way that gives rise to that situation, and then we just give ourselves a pat on the back for we believe we are right instead of realizing that our mind created a situation that made us act in a way that actually was the reason why the situation became a reality.

Let's say you are starting a new business. A friend of yours tells you that you are crazy to do so because he has heard many small business owners never succeed and end up losing it all. You assume that he is right and now become fearful of giving it your all, since, well, you do not want to lose it all. Instead of putting your 100% to this new business, you decide to stay in your current job and put the rest of your effort into your new business. You also do not spend a lot on advertising and other requirements since you assume the business will fail. Guess what? Your business will probably fail, but not because all small business fail, but rather because of the actions you took. Not giving it your 100% did not give it the energy and attention it deserved. Calls were not answered, products didn't come on time, you didn't hire the right employees, and not spending on advertising just made it very hard for people to know that your business was even there! Now let's switch things around: imagine you hear from a very successful friend of yours that he has seen growth in small business revenue and overall success. You believe him and assume he is right, so you decide to jump in with both feet. You spend all your time making sure that everything is running smoothly, you invest in the right employees, the right marketing plan, and an advertising campaign because, although it is an investment, deep in your heart you assume you will succeed, so... YOU DO! Your assumption drives your action, which will create the result! Assume always the best and your will always act accordingly!

*No, it's not all about you.*

Now let's move these assumptions into the personal world. Let's say you go to the teller to cash a check. She is making you do all this paperwork. She is short with you and not very pleasant. You assume she is just incredibly rude and obviously a bad person. Now every time you come to the bank you automatically close off, become very short and even rude yourself, and you basically hate going to this bank because you have to see this horrible person. What you might not know is that this teller has a very sick kid in the hospital. She doesn't sleep very much and, being a single mum, she can't take off work to be with her son. Now I am making this all up, but what I want to point out to you is that we also carry these negative assumptions even in our relationships and, unfortunately, we take everything personally, so this is another way in which we create more suffering for ourselves. In fact, the more self-centered you are, the more you will suffer, because you will take everything personally and everything will revolve around you and how you feel. If your friend can't make it to your birthday party because she has a situation, your reaction is not only that you will miss her but also one of asking yourself, "How can she do this to me?" When you go anywhere, you will be super worried about how you look and how you present yourself, because "I wonder what they will think of me?" Anything that happens, you take it personally when it is not! Newsflash, most people are too involved with their own egos to be spending any time worrying about yours. So let go, realize that not everything is about you, assume the best, the best of the situation, the best of an interaction, and see how your life changes! Things that you usually would carry for weeks will become meaningless. Nights thinking and overthinking, "How could this person do this to me?" and "Why would a person do that and be like that?" will be freed up for you to actually sleep or read a book. Isn't that nice? Letting go of your assumption that everything is about you will give you a sense of freedom that you have never experienced before! The less of your ego you have in your life, the more present the true you can become. No masks to protect yourself, no shows, you in your full splendor, in your full vulnerability, you will see then how many more open doors you will find and how many more smiling faces you will see. For what we are, we project, and what we think, we become!

## Food for thought... literally

Learning how to see the world differently requires some work. It is like rewiring your whole brain to create new impulses in different areas of the brain. We need to learn what we are doing wrong that keeps us creating negative, fearful, ego-based thoughts and what can we replace them with in order to create new pathways in the brain. The more we practice a thought, the quicker it will happen the next time we are in the same situation. So, in our teller at the bank scenario, since you got angry the first five times the situation occurred, now you don't even have to be at the bank for her image in your mind to automatically prompt you to be angry, just like that. The more we practice a thought, the more solid our belief and faster our response will be to create negative as well as positive feelings.

With this in mind, imagine what you daily consume in your thoughts without consciously thinking about it. You turn on the TV and are fed anger, violence, fear, self-loathing, etc. on a daily basis! Ask yourself, who do you hang out with? Are they positive, optimistic, kind, generous, patient, and inspirational, or energy zappers, pessimistic, fear-driven, angry, greedy, and unkind?

What about the movies you like watching, or the books you enjoy reading? What music are you listening to? Is it full of anger, repression, pessimism, fear, judgment, hate? Everything you surround yourself with is having a huge impact on how you see your life and the actions you end up taking in creating it.

So, if you want a positive, happy, healthy life, surround yourself with what feeds that instead. Give your brain food that will nourish peace, contentment, and joy. Hang out with people that inspire you: the happy, the hopeful the positive. Turn your TV off and don't read the newspaper. Stop constantly checking social media, since this will only increase your sense of lack and comparison. Instead, take time to be silent, read inspiring books, watch movies and documentaries that are uplifting. Surround yourself with that which you wish to become, let it permeate your being, and slowly rise your frequency, for we attract not what we desire, but what we become!

## Gratitude, the Great Equalizer

Among all the Spiritual practices, this is the easiest and most transforming. If you truly want to see how your perception changes and you want to see reality for the first time, make gratitude your daily practice. Gratitude opens you to the gift of life. Practice it and you will see. It puts you in a space of abundance, it aligns you with Grace. It makes you receptive and aware. Don't you see that the mere fact that you breathe is a gift? Be grateful for the big as well as the small. Be grateful for the mundane and the sublime. No matter if you are rich or poor, thin or fat, a man or a woman, gratitude balances everything. Gratitude doesn't see separation, accomplishments, social class, education level, race, gender, religion, or sexual preference. Gratitude can be practiced by anyone, at any time, and the benefits are the same for all. A happier, more abundant, more open-hearted person. Gratitude has the ability to see abundance where we believe there is none, possibility in despair, and light in dark times. Practice gratitude as you wake up and just before you go to sleep and you will see! Like Meister Eckhart says: If the only prayer you ever say in your entire life is thank you, it will be enough. Make gratitude your prayer – try it! You will see how slowly your world will transform before your eyes, for when we change, the whole world around us changes!

## Exercise 1: Gratitude Journal

Every morning before you get up and every night before you go to sleep, write down three things you are grateful for. Do it for twenty-one days.

## Exercise 2: Negativity Diet

For one whole week, disconnect from TV, news, social media, and going to the movies. Spend time in nature, read inspiring books, and meditate instead.

## Exercise 3: No Complaining for seven days

For the next seven days, make a commitment to yourself that you will not complain, no matter the situation. Make sure that you tell a friend who can call you daily to keep you accountable. If you complain, you will need to start all over again.

## Client Success Story

Mary was a beautiful woman. She was successful, she dressed impeccably and carried herself with authority. She could be perceived as intimidating, and she came to me to deal with depression. You see, although Mary on the outside seemed to be in control and seemed to have everything she wanted, inside she felt alone and longed for friendships and a romantic relationship. Unfortunately for her, she could not see that her ego created a big wall between her and others. As we worked together in balancing her hormones, nourishing her body properly, and most importantly, working on her mindset, she began to slowly bring down her walls. She allowed herself to become vulnerable and realized how many of her beliefs were based around how showing vulnerability was a sign of weakness and how perfection was needed to be loved, and how this had made her into what others perceived as a robot and repressed who she really truly was. It wasn't easy, and it took some time, but eventually her walls came down. It was lovely to see her come into her true self, laughing often, becoming warmer, allowing for the beauty of imperfection be perfectly her. I am happy to report that now she is no longer depressed and is currently married with a four-year-old and a baby on the way! See, a lot of the time it is us who are standing between ourselves and our dreams, we just do not know it, so having someone to guide us out of our own self-created prison is absolutely necessary!

# Chapter Eight

## SECRET FIVE –
## "CHANGING THE WORLD"

*"All those who are unhappy in the world are so as a result of their desire for their own happiness. All those who are happy in the world are so as a result of their desire for the happiness of others."*

– Shantideva

*"I slept and dreamt that life was joy. I awoke and saw that life was service. I acted and behold, service was joy."*

– Rabindranath Tagore

And so it is that we come to the most important chapter of them all. As you start shedding the layers of your mind and your ego, you will start realizing that focusing on your happiness alone has no longevity, especially if your happiness is at the expense of someone else's. Why? Because we are all interconnected; in truth we belong to each other. Nothing in your life happens with the help of others. "But Michelle, I take care of myself, I do everything for myself!" Well, not entirely; look at your food. Someone had to sow and harvest it, someone else drove it to the factory where it was cleaned, prepared, and packaged, and then again someone else took it to your supermarket, where someone else stacked it so that you could just come up and pick it up. The same thing with your clothes and any product you use. Let's say we only worry about ourselves and our own problems. Slowly we will feel isolated, alone. The more separation we create between our needs and the needs of others, the more we will suffer. Everything we do has an impact on others and that impact will have an impact back on ourselves.

That is where the rule of Karma or the concept of "we reap what we sow" comes into play. Karma is not something bad, as a lot of people believe; your karma simply reflects the cause and effect of your actions. Karma is a concept in a lot of Eastern philosophies and even in Christianity, that all of your actions have a result, that there is a cause for every effect. Nothing in this world happens without a cause. So even when you think you are doing nothing, that doing nothing will have an effect. Now, we are conditioned to think of only the results and not think enough about what we are generating. If you start focusing in your intention and what you are generating, you don't need to worry about the results, for what you will reap will be in direct response to what you have sown. Now, the when and the how will be out of your control, but the result will always come. If you understand the principle of Karma then you will focus on your thoughts and actions to make sure that your thoughts and intentions are aligned to the result you wish to manifest. Think and act with a pure heart and happiness will follow! When we realize that our actions toward others will end up having an impact on ourselves, we become smarter and start focusing on others' happiness too.

## Developing Compassion

His holiness the Dalai Lama, the worldwide-loved Buddhist monk and head of the Tibetan people, calls this developing compassion and becoming intelligently Selfish!

Why? Because developing compassion will always ultimately benefit YOU.

So, if you want to be Selfish, keep being so, but do it intelligently, understand that by being kind and compassionate to others, kindness and compassion will come back to yourself – although you will always get better results if you do things purely from the intention of benefitting others, since you will not be expecting anything in return, which will avoid you being disappointed if you don't. Let's say you help someone with the assumption that she will help you back, yet when the time comes and you ask for help, she can't do it. You now feel angry and disappointed. But if you help someone out with the pure intention to help, then the result doesn't matter and if you get a thank you or she helps you when you need it, this becomes a gift to be grateful for! See how the ego can hide even in the noblest of circumstances?

Compassion means developing understanding for another person's situation. It means putting ourselves in another person's shoes. When we put ourselves in another person's shoes, we can understand other people's reactions and choices. This allows us to not take things so personally, therefore not being so angry or resentful. It causes us to think before instinctively reacting; it further pushes us to see ourselves in others, to see our suffering in others; it makes us realize that they, too, want happiness and do not want to suffer. They, just like us, are doing the best they can with what they know. Developing compassion is not just a gift to the person that is receiving it, but more so to the one that is giving it. Compassion will split your heart wide open. It will allow you to become who you are. It will break the prison of the ego that is separating you from your true joy and happiness. When you develop compassion, you will realize that the world is all yours already. You will realize how impactful your being can be just by being present. Compassion will allow you to take the focus away from your own suffering and you will realize how tiny it truly is compared to the suffering of the world. When the fire of compassion is awakened in your heart, you will realize your Truth, your Mission, and the Way.

## Serving as an Antidote for Pain

Once the fire of compassion is truly lit in your being, you won't be able to see people suffering without taking action. And by taking action I don't mean you need to become a missionary and move to Africa or Guatemala, although you can very well be moved to do so – and if you are, please do! What I mean is that if you see someone sad you might smile at them, if you see someone suffering in the street you might give them a silent prayer. I love going to the supermarket or running errands and just sporadically wishing people some compassion prayer. As they pass me by, I silently say, "May you be happy, may you be peaceful, may you be free from suffering!" Try it – it is truly life changing. Whenever you are suffering, instead of dwelling on your own misery think of someone who might be suffering too and pray for them, send them a good thought, or, more than that, call them or offer them help. Finding solace from your suffering by helping someone else is not only a great way of breaking your Self-focus and making things even bigger (remember, what we focus on grows), but it will also help you accumulate good karma and will make you feel good, too! It has been proven that serotonin, or the "feel good hormone," is released when we are the recipients and the givers of kindness; in fact, just watching an act of kindness will have the same effect!

Now I know suffering is something none of us want to go through, yet pain is the other side of happiness and there can't be one without the other. Just like we need darkness to appreciate the light, so do we need suffering to cherish the blessings. More so, pain can be a way of transforming, of bringing out the best in us. In yoga, we call this "Rajas," or purification by fire. Wanted or not, believe it or not, you are going through a Spiritual journey, and suffering is one of the ways our Spirit purifies and grows. Let's say you ask God for patience; what do you think God will do to give you patience? You will be put in situations where you will need to practice patience, and that is how your patience will grow. Want to prove your faith? Then my love, show your faith in the dark times. That is when you truly show faith and when your faith really has a chance to grow. A person's character is truly apparent when they are going through struggle. So, fight the fight with dignity, with acceptance. Let go and let God. Surrender to what is and the struggle will be over. Become receptive to Grace and allow for the miracle to happen. The miracle is not outside you, or for the pain to disappear – the miracle is YOU, through this pain transforming and breaking down the walls of your ego, of your hate, of your fear of the delusion. So don't let the pain and the fear and anxiety stop you and paralyze you. For that which won't leave you alone, that which won't let you sleep, is what is calling you back. It is trying to remind you of who you are and what you are here for! Do not numb it with pills, do not quiet it with noise, do not be afraid. For you, my darling, came here with your own melody, with your own song. Question it, be silent, and listen to what it has to say. There, deeply hidden in your heart, is the joy you have been searching for!

Become receptive to Grace. Let the walls of the temple of your heart be torn down so you can be you in ALL your glory and receive the gifts the Universe has waiting for you!

Many years ago, I went to hear a Sufi teacher speak, and she said that many times we act like children in a candy store. We have tantrums because we want a particular candy and grasp it so tightly because we do not want it to go, yet if we just would loosen our grip, we might realize God wants to give us the whole candy store – but because we are holding on so tight, we do not have an empty hand to receive it. In life sometimes, we want to believe we know better than that which created us – call it God, the Universe, Intelligence – yet since the womb you have been taken care of by no other than life itself. Now, as adults, we want to decide what is best for ourselves and sometimes, okay, many times, we close ourselves to the possibilities of the greater plan. Sometimes the doors that close are for our own benefit. Sometimes getting a NO is the greatest gift you will ever have, yet you don't know it and since you can't see it, since you can't see the big picture, you fight, you struggle, and you suffer, yet if you would fully surrender to the Grace that brought you here, you might be surprised by how easily you will be carried on wings to the wonderful life that you are really meant to live. Becoming receptive to

Grace means opening yourself up to possibilities that some things are not in your own grasping. Becoming receptive to Grace means starting to connect the dots, trusting that things are working in your favor ALWAYS, and that the Universe wants you to succeed.

Once you open yourself to Grace and decide not just to ask from it but to serve it, you will find it will serve you and all the things that you have so desperately been running around for, have been struggling for, will easily come to you. When we become aligned with what we came from, we don't struggle anymore. You will see that from your own transformation. Relationships that were difficult before now will become easier and even seem warm and drama free. The finances you kept struggling with will all of a sudden just start flowing in. You, too, will start flowing and vibrating with the Universe, just like catching a wave and being supported by it, with no struggle and no fight.

Now, from my personal journey and what I have seen in my patients, the final frontier to truly becoming receptive to Grace and abandoning your fear, is finding meaning.

Now, a lot of people believe that finding meaning means getting something or becoming someone "important" or doing something extraordinary, and that is where everything fails and we set ourselves up for failure and unhappiness. Once again, we look outside for that meaning, when the meaning is within us. Even drinking a cup of tea can become quite meaningful if we decide to make it so. We believe for a relationship to be meaningful there have to be fireworks all the time, but a truly meaningful relationship, for example, is the one that discovers the magic in the ordinary, the one that doesn't last just a couple of months but that finds beauty in the wrinkles of another, whose beauty in their heart has surpassed the physical form. A job can be meaningful even if it touches just one person and your intention is of serving and loving no matter what you do.

I remember the story of a toll worker who loved her work. People noticed because she always was happy and kind to everyone who passed by her tollbooth. She mentioned that it was her opportunity to make a difference in the world just by smiling in the early morning when everyone was rushed and in a bad mood. See, you can find your meaning right now, just by deciding to do so, by becoming mindful of your intention and making a conscious decision to choose to serve others as much as you can, that you want to make your life count. Now even washing the dishes can become an act of service and we can do it joyfully. All the things that you do not like in your life can be transformed by this mere fact. Learn how to serve the world and the world and joy will be yours, no matter what is going on outside yourself. For the ultimate way to find true happiness and freedom is by serving others, for in the service of others you will find meaning and ultimately lasting and joyful peace.

## Exercise 1: Volunteer

Find something you are passionate about – it could be a breast cancer association, pet adoption center, foster kids... anything that moves you – and volunteer to help in any way you can.

## Exercise 2: Practice No Meat Monday

Consciously deciding to not eat meat for one day a week greatly impacts the well-being of the earth as well as the lives of wonderful little animals. If you are not ready to jump onto the vegetarian wagon but you still want to make a difference with your eating habits, this is a great start! Visit **https://www.meatfreemondays.com/** for more info on how it benefits everyone, including you and your health!

## Exercise 3: Pay it Forward

Pay for someone else's toll, groceries, or coffee without their noticing and see the chain reaction of kindness and goodness you might just ignite!

## Exercise 4: Adopt a Pet

Nothing brings more joy than a pet. Many pet adopters, like myself, say that they did not save the pet but that the pet saved them. I know that this is a much more extreme commitment than the other exercises, yet if you are feeling lonely and have the time, finances, and heart to do it, adopting a pet might just change your life forever!

## Client Success Story

James came to me with terrible sciatica pain. He was an older gentleman with a very stiff body and a very mean personality to go with it – or at least, others thought so. James smoked like a chimney, was an alcoholic, and wasn't terribly popular at his job. He was not really friendly, and he had a way that would repel most people. Yet under that tough exterior, I recognized a gentle kind soul, desperate for love and connection. As we started working together, I suggested that he to try my gentle yoga class. He laughed at the idea of it. I also invited him to our Spiritual Circle, where we would read inspiring books and later comment on the lessons. The first time he came to was a true battle. He kept arguing and questioning everything I said. It wasn't easy, but I knew it wasn't really him, it was his ego desperate to survive. You should have seen his face when I asked him to come back and told him what a pleasure it had been to have him there. He couldn't believe it! But sure enough, he came back. Encouraged by others in the group, he finally decided to do the yoga classes. It was tough for him – he was really rigid and obviously hadn't exercised in a long time – yet he gave it his all. And he kept giving it his all for months.

By this time people were starting to see what I already knew: James was one of a kind. He would not miss yoga class for anything in the world. His appearance completely changed, he became kinder, softer. He, who had been a stickler about money, now would invite us all to dinner after Friday yoga! He smiled with his whole being now. Obviously, his sciatica pain disappeared, but to his wife's amazement he stopped drinking, too! See, he found peace inside himself, so he could deal with things better. People now approached him, and he felt loved and connected. Long gone was the old unhappy, angry James. Now there was only James... and he was happy.

# CHAPTER NINE

## HABITS ARE STRONGER THAN GOOD INTENTIONS

*"A Precious Human Life"*

*Every day,*

*think as you wake up*

*Today I am fortunate*

*to have woken up.*

*I am alive,*

*I have a precious human life.*

*I am not going to waste it.*

*I am going to use all my energies to develop myself,*

*to expand my heart out to others,*

*to achieve enlightenment for the*
*benefit of all beings.*
*I am going to have kind thoughts towards others*
*I am not going to get angry, or think*
*badly about others.*
*I am going to benefit others as much as I can."*
– His Holiness the XIVth Dalai Lama

So, now is your time to come out of the darkness and shine! You have been given the secret keys to start opening the doors that have kept you prisoner and it is only you who can open them! Now, do not be afraid, for change takes time and fearless determination! But now you know the way and there is so much deeper to go and so much more to learn.

I do not want to tell you that everything is going to be easy from now on and that you might not stumble back on to your old ways. We all do! In fact, one of my teachers told me once, "Michelle, habits are stronger than good intentions."

How true her words were, for sometimes, although we want change so desperately, we can succumb to our old habits and patterns quiet easily, plus our ego will show us time and time again reasons to not move forward. In fact, fear, the very thing we are trying to avoid, will be the first thing that might pop up – but remember, facing that fear is what will empower you to become the person that you truly are and to achieve your goal of long-lasting joy. So, when fear starts to paralyze you and push you back to your old ways, my darling, don't be discouraged. Don't talk down to yourself and never ever give up. The goal of true joy is too precious to let go! Also, be prepared for your outer world to start changing and to face some resistance, not only from yourself but from others close to you. I remember that as I went through my own transformation and started vibrating with a higher energy, my old friends started to get upset at me for not drinking with them, or not going to parties, etc. I remember all of a sudden a new male prospect would come along to deter me from my goal – and yes, sometimes I fell back into the cycle of suffering, to be chewed, swallowed, and regurgitated again, but this time I knew better and the more this happened, the more I knew I had to stick to my higher goal. All of a sudden, I started meeting new and wonderful friends who were also on the same journey I was. New doors started opening as well and yes, as you imagine, I also found the love of my life in the most magical and unexpected way – but that is a whole new story and you will be able to read it in my next book, *The Energetics of Love*. But I digress. The better your practice and the closer you are to your goal, the more these offbeat events will start popping up. These are just a test – in fact, they are a sure way to prove that you are making progress – but when they do appear, keep going like a horse with blinders. Do not get distracted from your goal. Come back over and over to this book and, like I said before, if you need reinforcements I am right here.

Yet, if you do get pushed off of the highway of transformation by a huge truck of old habits, take a deep breath and once again make your way back on to the road. This road will take you to the so desired goal where you will leave your anxiety and depression behind for good, so don't give up. With fearless determination, get back on the road and try again! This book and I will be here to support you, no matter what. Without judgment, without analyzing or beating yourself down, just get back to the practice and realize success is one step closer with every failure. Becoming who you are meant to be in all your greatness is the best gift you can give to yourself and to anyone you love. And it is the best way you can show gratitude to that which created you!

Now, there are proven ways to help you sustain your goal and keep you accountable. One is by practice. Day in and day out, make practice your daily goal. Practice, practice, practice. This is the only way to achieve your goal. Make sure you do all the exercises and that you do them daily. This way you are creating new habits that in turn will create new actions that will create new results. Be aware of your thoughts, for they dictate your action. Remember that what we think so shall we become, so at the beginning, fake it until you make it!

Another sure way of making your new lessons truly stick with you is finding a teacher. It is said that, "When the student is ready, the teacher will appear," and you ARE READY!

Finding the right teacher is as important as the practice itself, for the wrong teacher can lead you even further from the Truth, while the true teacher will only get you closer to your Self, which ultimately is the true teacher; however, in the process, having an external teacher who has walked the talk and who will not only guide you but keep you accountable can make you get to your goal a lot faster and with much more ease. I find that all my clients and patients have found this to be true. So if you would like for me to hold your hand and for me to show you the way into the beauty, power, health, and peace that you already are, remember that you can always reach out to me directly. Shoot me a note at **info@theenergeticsofjoy.com** and we'll see if working together might make the difference in your finally finding your way and sticking to it!

So, when the thoughts of "I don't have the time to make all these changes" or "I do not have the money to invest in a coach or a teacher," comes up, know that all of these are excuses from your old self and your ego to not let you move forward into the person you are about to become. Remember, you can do this! You are the one you have been looking for. Become fearless in your determination to break free from your fear-based prison and discover the joy that already resides inside you as you!

# CHAPTER TEN

## CONCLUSION

With this, we come to the last chapter in this book and, at the same time, to the first chapter of the rest of your life. I wish for you all the Joy, Peace, and Love that you already are and above all I wish you to have fearless determination so that out of this pain can come something beautiful and majestic... YOU. Just like the phoenix, coming out of the ashes, so too you will soar to even higher and brighter heights than you ever imagined possible! So just like the wise Taoist sage Lao Tzu said, "The journey of a thousand miles starts with one step," so you too take a step at a time. Remember that this world we are currently living in pushes us to become crazy hamsters in a wheel and that the fruit of happiness promised through their methods is a sure way to trap us in the wheel of suffering – yet you can step off at any point, and the best time to start doing it is now.

Also, when we begin our path of transformation, the only way to do it permanently is by starting with a strong and powerful base, and that base is unapologetic and ruthless Self-Love and kindness. Cultivate this love for yourself. Start practicing the exercises in Chapter 5 and see how out of this deep love for yourself will come fearless determination to stop your own suffering!

Whenever tired or physically depleted, revisit Chapter 6 and make sure you are taking care of your body, which is the vessel of your beautiful Soul. Balancing the body and making sure you understand how the energy of the body works will have a great impact on the energy you bring to yourself and others and it will help carry you victoriously on the journey to your mighty goal of permanent joy!

Cultivate a beautiful mind and you will reap a beautiful life. Go to Chapter 7 and make sure you are watering the right seeds in your mind, so your thoughts will be beautiful roses in the garden of life!

Finally, give yourself wholeheartedly to Grace. Go back to Chapter 8 and rediscover how, by serving others and trusting that the Universe has your back, not only will you find your ultimate meaning and purpose by making your life a beautiful work of art, but you will become, like

St. Francis, a joyful prayer that the world will sing...

*"Lord, make me an instrument of Your peace.*

*Where there is hatred, let me sow love;*

*where there is injury, pardon;*

*where there is doubt, faith;*

*where there is despair, hope;*

*where there is darkness, light;*

*where there is sadness, joy.*

*O, Divine Master, grant that I may not so much seek to be consoled as to console;*

*to be understood as to understand;*

*to be loved as to love;*

*For it is in giving that we receive; it is in pardoning that we are pardoned; it is in dying that we are born again to eternal life."*

– St Francis of Assisi

# ACKNOWLEDGMENTS

To the Unconditional Love I come from: Thank you for the gift of this precious life. Thank you for all the love, the kindness, the beauty, and the joy.

Thank you for sustaining me, for supporting me, for carrying me on your ever-so-gentle and nurturing wings, may my every breath and effort be a prayer of gratitude towards your Infinite Love.

To His Holiness the Dalai Lama, the Ocean of Compassion who broke open the wall of my heart and mind and awakened in me the desire of all Bodhisattvas.

To my beloved teacher Shri Dharma Mittra for his infinite compassion towards me and for showing me through his teachings and example the way of Love, Fortitude, and Angry Determination in order to achieve the Ultimate Goal of Self-Realization.

To my beloved sons, Noah and baby Shane, for their unwavering support and understanding, for the many days and nights they accepted being away from their mommy so I could finish this book. This book is for you boys.

May it contribute to leaving a better, kinder world for you, my boys, and may you by reading it become better, kinder humans for this world.

To my darling husband, Anthony, who, for days and nights a plenty, stayed with two tired, hungry, and crying little boys after work so I could write this book. From the beginning, he has been my biggest and most supportive fan and has encouraged me to follow this dream.

And to my first and greatest teachers, who throughout my life have shown me nothing but love, kindness, and compassion, my parents Carlos and Chiqui, "Los amo con todo mi corazon y les agradezco todo el amor y apoyo que siempre me han dado."

To each and every client and patient who has trusted me with their health and their hearts, thank you. Being able to show you your own beauty and Light has been and forever will be the privilege of my life.

And to you, my beloved reader, thank you so much for trusting me with your vulnerability and receptiveness. May this book help you breathe a little bit easier, and may it become a catalyst of inspiration for your own path to healing and Ultimate Joy.

# About the Author

DR. EGGENBERGER was born in Guatemala City and moved to the United States when she was only eighteen years old to study and search for a better life.

She attained a bachelor's degree at the University of Miami and after some personal health concerns decided to give her life a 180-degree change. She went back to school and now she has a bachelor's degree in Health Studies and a Master's in Oriental Medicine from AMC college in Florida.

She is a Doctor of Oriental Medicine and Licensed Acupuncture Physician, certified by the National Commission of Oriental Medicine and the State of Florida.

She studied under the personal guidance of Dr. Gordon Xu and is a certified Health Coach of Integrative Nutrition from Sunny University in New York and a certified 800-hour Yoga teacher of both Kripalu Yoga and Dharma Yoga.

She became a regular presenter on national television, appearing in *Nuestro Mundo por la Mañana* and *Matutino Express por Canal Antigua*, bringing the best of natural medicine to Guatemala. She has also been on national radio programs "Urban Health" on Radio Infinita and Radio Sonora and inspired people to be happier and healthier with the program "Domingo de Despertares" (Sundays of Awakenings).

Dr. Eggenberger has had successful practices in Miami, Australia, and Guatemala. At the end of 2017, family reasons had her move again – now to Orlando and the beautiful city of Lake Mary, where she currently lives with her husband, Anthony, and her two sons, Noah and Shane.

Website:
**www.theenergeticsofjoy.com**
**www.dreggenberger.com**
**www.dharmaclinicfl.com**
Email: **info@theenergeticsofjoy.com**
Facebook: Dr. Michelle Eggenberger (Prema Om)
Michelle Eggenberger (Dharma Clinic/lakemary)

# ABOUT DIFFERENCE PRESS

Difference Press offers entrepreneurs, including life coaches, healers, consultants, and community leaders, a comprehensive solution to get their books written, published, and promoted. A boutique-style alternative to self-publishing, Difference Press boasts a fair and easy-to-understand profit structure, low-priced author copies, and author-friendly contract terms. Its founder, Dr. Angela Lauria, has been bringing to life the literary ventures of hundreds of authors-in-transformation since 1994.

---

## LET'S MAKE A DIFFERENCE WITH YOUR BOOK

You've seen other people make a difference with a book. Now it's your turn. If you are ready to stop watching and start taking massive action, reach out.

"Yes, I'm ready!"

In a market where hundreds of thousands books are published every year and are never heard from again, all participants of The Author Incubator have bestsellers that are actively changing lives and making a difference.

"In two years we've created over 250 bestselling books in a row, 90% from first-time authors." We do this by selecting the highest quality and highest potential applicants for our future programs.

Our program doesn't just teach you how to write a book—our team of coaches, developmental editors, copy editors, art directors, and marketing experts incubate you from book idea to published bestseller, ensuring that the book you create can actually make a difference in the world. Then we give you the training you need to use your book to make the difference you want to make in the world, or to create a business out of serving your readers. If you have life-or world-changing ideas or services, a servant's heart, and the willingness to do what it REALLY takes to make a difference in the world with your book, go to http://theauthorincubator.com/apply/ to complete an application for the program today.

# OTHER BOOKS BY DIFFERENCE PRESS

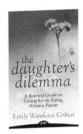

The Daughter's Dilemma: A Survival Guide to Caring for an Aging, Abusive Parent

by Emily Wanderer Cohen

Trumpcare v. Obamacare: How to Shop for Health Care in the Chaos

by Jennifer Dailey

Eat the Berries: Weight Loss for Busy Moms

by Jamie Patterson Hernandez

From Invisible to Visible: Master the Art of Being Seen

by Rhonda Kaalund

Thrive at the Top: The CEO's Guide to Chronic Pain Relief by Ken Malloy

Riches for Real Estate Agents: Have, Be, and Do Everything You Want by Jarett Shaffer and Susan Shaffer

Slay the Dragon: Self-Empowerment and Renewal for First Responders by Dr. Kathleen Tallent

The Art of Romance: Love, Sex, and Dating on Your Own Terms by Reverend Stephanie Wild

# THANK YOU

Thank you again for buying this book and for being receptive to Grace!

Remember to go to **www.theenergeticsofjoy.com/elementquiz** and you will get a better idea of what your energetic constitution is and what element you need to balance – and how!

Also, I would love to hear what you thought or if you have any questions. To reach out, please go to **info@theenergeticsofjoy.com.**

If you would like a FREE STRATEGY SESSION to see where you are at and how and what you can do to faster and make more permanent change in your life, send me an email at **info@theenergeticsofjoy.com.**